T0098791

FROM BREAKDOWN TO BREAKTHROUGH

FROM BREAKDOWN
TO
BREAKTHROUGH

Forging Resilient
Business Relationships
in the Heat of Change

MICHAEL PAPANEK
with Liz Alexander, PhD

New York

FROM BREAKDOWN TO BREAKTHROUGH
Forging Resilient Business Relationships in the Heat of Change

© 2017 **MICHAEL PAPANEK** .

All rights reserved. No portion of this book may be reproduced, stored in a retrieval system, or transmitted in any form or by any means—electronic, mechanical, photocopy, recording, scanning, or other—except for brief quotations in critical reviews or articles, without the prior written permission of the publisher.

Published in New York, New York, by Morgan James Publishing. Morgan James and The Entrepreneurial Publisher are trademarks of Morgan James, LLC. www.MorganJamesPublishing.com

The Morgan James Speakers Group can bring authors to your live event. For more information or to book an event visit The Morgan James Speakers Group at www.TheMorganJamesSpeakersGroup.com.

Shelfie

A **free** eBook edition is available with the purchase of this print book.

CLEARLY PRINT YOUR NAME ABOVE IN UPPER CASE

Instructions to claim your free eBook edition:
1. Download the Shelfie app for Android or iOS
2. Write your name in **UPPER CASE** above
3. Use the Shelfie app to submit a photo
4. Download your eBook to any device

ISBN 978-1-63047-980-0 paperback
ISBN 978-1-63047-981-7 eBook
ISBN 978-1-63047-982-4 hardcover
Library of Congress Control Number: 2016902552

Cover Design by:
Rachel Lopez
www.r2cdesign.com

Interior Design by:
Bonnie Bushman
The Whole Caboodle Graphic Design

In an effort to support local communities and raise awareness and funds, Morgan James Publishing donates a percentage of all book sales for the life of each book to Habitat for Humanity Peninsula and Greater Williamsburg.

Get involved today, visit
www.MorganJamesBuilds.com

Habitat for Humanity®
Peninsula and
Greater Williamsburg
Building Partner

This book is dedicated to my mother Miriam Lewin,
my father George Papanek, and my son Daniel Papanek.
I miss you.

CONTENTS

ACKNOWLEDGEMENTS

The premise of this book is that one's overall success is based on the relationships that you build over your entire career, rather than just your own skills and capabilities. Without others, we can accomplish nothing of real value. This book is certainly no exception.

If you are one of my colleagues, either from back in my EDS (Electronic Data Systems) days, through my years at Interaction Associates, to today, please know you have been an invaluable teacher to me. Everything I know about leadership I have gathered from your examples and every difficulty I faced I overcame with your help. I believe in the power of leadership because of you. I would never have completed this book without your training, trust, creativity, support, and encouragement. Thank you for the thousands of hours of thinking, working, and talking together.

I would like to thank the many leaders in organizations large and small who have given me the privilege of working with them to improve their lives on the job. I have been honored that you would help me develop the ideas in this book by applying them with your teams. Thank you for showing the way and allowing me to learn with you. Kurt Lewin believed our theories are only valuable if they help people in the real world. I hope this book provides practical tools you and your teams can use to be even more successful.

A very special thank you to my co-author and writing coach extraordinaire, Dr. Liz Alexander. Liz is a very special person, deeply good hearted and truly gifted, not only as an author and businessperson, but also as a partner—in the very best sense of the word. This book is much better than it would have been without you (and it might not exist at all)! I learned so much from you. Knowing you were always there to help kept me going.

My editing partner, Bess Lovejoy, was invaluable in managing the process of making my ideas work on the written page without losing my voice. Thank you so much for your help. Priya Kumar's graphics were perfect and you are so easy to work with—even from thousands of miles away.

I would especially like to thank the leaders who agreed to be interviewed and quoted in the book; they have contributed greatly to the value of the book for our readers, and I am grateful for their generosity and openness.

Thank you to everyone at Morgan James for your entrepreneurial spirit and your trust in a first-time author.

Thank you to Khalid Halim, Dave Motto, and Alan Armstrong for your coaching, brainstorming, research, feedback, and so much more. Your help in understanding the connections between resilience, change, and leadership leaves me in your debt. I am lucky to have such smart friends who are also such great leaders.

Thank you to Sebastian for keeping me company through the many hours.

To my wife Robyn, and my daughters Kathryn and Julia, thank you for your never-ending positive support and for not asking me when the book would be done too often. Extra thanks to Kathryn and her husband Jared for your help with the text. Double extra thanks to Robyn for being so understanding on all those weekends I spent on "The Book" and not with you.

This book is written in honor of my grandfather Kurt Lewin.

INTRODUCTION

August 8, 2008 (8/8/08), seemed an auspicious date on which to launch myself as a self-employed consultant. So it was with positive anticipation that I left the firm where I'd worked for more than sixteen years to set up my own consulting practice. The enormity of the change—and the challenge—was not lost on me. I kept my spirits high and my confidence fired up by thinking about what I had to bring to the table: over twenty years of experience as a leadership and organizational change consultant with a strong resume, a reputation as a rainmaker, and a wealth of contacts. There was also the possibility of working for my old firm as an independent consultant, and at much higher rates.

Twenty-three days later, Lehman Brothers filed for the largest bankruptcy in US history. The New York Stock Exchange fell more than seven hundred points in one day. Commentators were predicting that ATMs might stop working and that we would all be "eating grass" within a week.

Had I just made the biggest mistake of my professional career?

As the initial shock began to wear off, I realized that what I had always taken for granted was now in jeopardy. My former business life had been like driving a speedboat along an easily navigable river: no obstacles, full speed ahead. Now it seemed as if the water level had dropped precariously, exposing all the rocks, garbage, and other barriers that had always been there but that I'd never had to consciously consider before. I started to doubt whether my business relationships were strong enough to allow me to navigate in this new, uncertain environment.

I wondered: had I always been fair to others in my business dealings? Did I really try hard enough to produce results that benefited everyone, or was the focus more on my needs? I knew I had the skills, but did I have a *good-enough* reputation to weather this new storm?

Because my old company used a group of independent consultants as contract workers to meet shifting client needs, I'd assumed they'd send work my way while I built my own practice. However, my fears grew as I realized my former colleagues had many independent consultants to choose from and, now, less work to farm out to them. Why would they choose me?

As I took a long, hard look at my current business relationships, I realized that too many of them were in *breakdown* mode—meaning they were not as positive, solid, or likely to survive these challenging times as I needed them to be. In fact, some of the relationships at my old firm had been so dysfunctional that they had largely influenced my decision to move on. Now that everyone was experiencing enormous stress in the wake of what was to be known as the Great Recession, many of these relationships appeared to be too tenuous to survive this new "normal." What I needed was a way to transform them from *breakdown* to *breakthrough*.

You may have experienced something similar. Whether starting your own business or adapting to today's uncertainty and rapid change, perhaps you have also found that stress has detrimentally impacted your business relationships?

Let's face it: our hyper-connected world has profoundly changed the rules of business engagement. The higher up the hierarchy we go, the less inclined we may be to adapt quickly to a more cooperative, collaborative way of interacting. After all, isn't that what leadership is about, according to popular culture? Getting people to buy into *our* vision, directing them to do what *we* want, being wholly focused on what "I" need to achieve?

You Don't Need "Connections," You Need Relationships

The idea that relationships matter in business is not new. Some of the most successful companies of our time are really relationship stories: Hewlett and Packard; Jobs and Wozniak; Gates and Allen. The impact of broken relationships is also clear. Think of the conflicts at the heart of breakdowns at Yahoo! (Carol Bartz versus Yahoo!'s board of directors); Apple (Sculley versus Jobs in the 1990s); and General Motors (Roger Smith versus Ross Perot in the 1980s). Long gone are the days when leaders could expect to gain respect through the unabashed exercise of power alone. Now we see successful leaders who have implemented new products and grown revenues and profits, but then were removed from their positions because of their inability to work effectively with others.

For example, consider the resignation in 2012 of Steven Sinofsky, a twenty-three-year veteran executive of Microsoft who many thought was next in line for a top job at that organization. Sinofsky had successfully brought Windows 8 and the new Microsoft tablet to market but had to resign because of his poor relationships with other executives—a leadership brand that other Microsoft employees described as "ruthless." Without strong relationships with other employees, Sinofsky's wildly successful business outcomes were not enough to protect him once his key benefactor, Bill Gates, left Microsoft. Sinofsky had been "winning" according to the old leadership model, but the heat and stress he created had burned bridges along the way. While he had a great relationship with Gates, that was not the case with Microsoft overall.

The conclusion to draw from this example isn't that leaders should try to eliminate any conflict or "heat." Successful teams benefit from diversity of thinking, and there will always be some degree of conflict evident within powerful teams. Indeed, we do need *some* degree of tension to stimulate creativity and innovation. But when the head of sales can't get along with the head of marketing, or one fiefdom within the organization is always at odds with another, the effect not only potentially impacts customers, clients, and investors—this friction also takes its toll on the employees caught in the crossfire.

The secret lies in having *resilient* working relationships. But what do I mean by that?

Have you ever tried sitting on a rickety old or poorly manufactured chair? Maybe it needs repairing or had never been designed properly to begin with; you just know you can't rely on it. If you are stuck having to use the chair, you always sit down carefully, knowing it's unwise to put all your weight on it. It's nerve-racking every time, because you're always wondering if you're going to end up sprawled on the floor.

This is analogous to many business relationships today. A weak business relationship is not designed to hold the "weight" generated by the continual stress and strain of work.

On the other hand, a resilient relationship is like a solid, totally reliable chair, one you know you can confidently sink into when the stress of a long day has worn you out or when you need to get some focused work done. No matter how much weight or pressure you put on that chair, it's constructed well enough to ensure you always feel fully supported.

Relationships Under Stress

Though we recovered from the 2008 meltdown, continuing crisis, such as the US government shutdown and near-default, show that the world has changed. In our new "VUCA" world (volatile, uncertain, complex, ambiguous), relationships are even more important. When the everyday assumptions we make at work are changing quickly, we need to know we can count on our colleagues; that we are all in this together. Too often, change and stress can cause us to attack, protect ourselves, and pull away from one another. This behavior reinforces a vicious cycle of isolation, conflict, and fear, causing relationships to break down and important business projects and goals to fail.

Take a look at some of the results that show the importance of relationships in today's stressful work environment:

- 41 percent of employees are stressed (American Psychological Association).[1]
- 71 percent of employees are not engaged—worse yet, this number has barely moved over twelve years of surveys (Gallup).[2]
- Managers are almost as disengaged as employees—with only 35 percent engaged—and through their negative impact, Gallup estimates that managers who are not engaged or who are actively disengaged cost the US economy $319 billion to $398 billion annually (Gallup).[3]
- Employees do not leave an *organization*; they leave their *poor relationships* with their bosses (Buckingham & Coffman, Gallup).[4]

---

1   American Psychological Association, Stress in America 2009, accessed June 11, 2014, http://www.apa.org/news/press/releases/stress-exec-summary.pdf.
2   "State of the American Manager," Gallup, 2015.
3   "State of the American Manager," Gallup, 2015.
4   Marcus Buckingham and Curt Coffman, First, Break All The Rules: What the World's Greatest Managers Do Differently (New York: Simon & Schuster, 1999), 33.

- Engagement with an organization is emotional and based on the sum of relationships with managers and other team members or partners (Conference Board).[5]
- Highly driven engineers say leaders with great technical skills are not enough, and that they also expect people skills from managers (Google Project Oxygen/*New York Times*).[6]

The main premise of this book is that we *are in charge* of our relationships, not subject to them. Only when we confront the unvarnished truth about our *own* power over our business relationships can we make a conscious choice to change them for the better.

A Rude Awakening

Remember I told you I was hoping to continue receiving assignments from my former firm? As luck would have it, within a short period of time I received a call from them, asking me to work on a project that focused on accelerating sales and lead generation, an area in which I excelled. Everything sounded wonderful until I was told who my key contact in the firm would be.

Let's call her Julie. She was someone with whom I'd had one of the most contentious relationships of my entire career. I felt, based on my past experience with her, that she was sometimes destructive, often seemed motivated by her own agenda, and I feared was actually incompetent in our field of organizational development. I had argued against the decision to hire her because of her lack of relevant background, then continued to disagree with most of her actions as she made her mark on the company. Now she held my contract in her hands and would be the one directing and evaluating my work!

5 Ann Barrett and John Beeson, Developing Business Leaders for 2010 (Conference Board, 2002).

6 Adam Bryant, "Google's Quest to Build a Better Boss," New York Times, March 12, 2011.

Without having the luxury of turning down a lucrative deal, I realized I could either fight a potentially losing battle with a person who spared no opportunity to show that she felt the same antipathy toward me—or I could try to make this relationship work. Changed economic circumstances forced me to think seriously about how I could achieve a breakthrough in this relationship, when we'd previously only experienced one breakdown after another. And I needed to make sure this happened quickly if my fledgling consulting business was to survive.

As I prepared for our first meeting together, I went through a thought process that I later developed into a unique breakthrough strategy.

First I asked myself: what was most important to this person? I knew that what Julie wanted above all else was results.

So did I, of course, but I began to recognize that we each had different approaches to achieving those outcomes. This had been a particular source of friction in our previous relationship. If I was going to make the relationship work now, I needed to focus on becoming more *flexible*. I needed to learn how to let go of my firmly held beliefs concerning Julie's ulterior motives and lack of skills. I promised myself that no matter what she said, I would find a way to be more accommodating.

As I forced myself to view my relationship with Julie more objectively and less emotionally—to look at it largely from Julie's point of view—I recognized how my behavior and attitude had conspired to plunge our relationship into breakdown mode. This realization did not sit well with me. Did I want to be someone who helped create a difficult situation and then, when things fell apart, blamed the intransigence of the other person? No! Although I had no way of knowing whether Julie would now be any more accommodating of my viewpoints than when we last met, at least I could control what *I* did. If this relationship were to fall apart again, at least I would know that I'd been *flexible* enough to give it a real, honest try.

Next, I wondered what else I might need to understand about Julie. Looking back, I could see that she had been frustrated that we'd not been able to combine our considerable talents to become an effective and successful team. I committed to *strengthening* our relationship by finding ways in which we could multiply each other's value and contributions.

Finally, I turned the focus even more deeply inward, to ask: what was my real intention here? In what ways did I have a tendency to espouse my values and expect others to live up to them, but not do so myself?

I had always thought of myself as an honest, hardworking person and I felt good when I helped and supported others. It was time for me to live up to this ideal of myself, not just with those with whom I found it easy to get along, but with a person I'd found very difficult to collaborate with in the past. I committed to going into that first meeting with Julie and—while I wouldn't pretend the past had never happened—giving her agenda a *fair* hearing, showing respect, and being prepared for some give-and-take.

Thinking Is Not Enough

Many of you might consider my decision to improve my relationship with Julie to be all the preparation necessary to change my long-held beliefs about her, and sufficient enough to allow me to work with her more smoothly. But it isn't! Just thinking about what you intend to do isn't enough, especially if you make a one-off decision to act differently and then set the decision aside until the event or experience actually takes place.

That's why I didn't stop with my decision to view my relationship with Julie differently. Instead, before our first meeting I visualized a series of responses from her so I could rehearse how I would react and wouldn't be caught off-guard when we were face-to-face. I imagined her making comments during our meeting, saw myself listening, nodding in assent, and saying yes to her suggestions.

But I knew that would only get me so far. After all, I had to prepare myself for consequences I didn't like and suggestions with which I didn't agree. I had to also picture myself reacting more optimally at times when, deliberately or unconsciously, Julie caused a strong negative reaction in me, as I expected her to do.

In order to help myself respond favorably to Julie's behavior, I trained myself to focus on what it was I intended to achieve in this relationship. It was important for me to continually ask: what is the true goal here? It wasn't to "win" over Julie, but for us to work together to grow sales for my old firm.

Double-Loop Learning

What I needed to practice is called "double-loop" learning. Single-loop, or simple, learning essentially means accepting the status quo and optimizing what you are already doing. This is good enough if the task is simple—such as baking a cake—and your current approach seems to be working pretty well (next time, just a tad more vanilla, for example).

However, most real change requires double-loop learning. Double-loop learning occurs when you question your current assumptions, beliefs, and values so you can try something new and achieve more dramatic impact. To be successful in this more complex situation, I knew I needed to be willing to learn and change at a deeper level. I even role-played my conversation with Julie in advance with someone I knew well and felt safe with.

Into the Heat

On the day of our meeting, I had barely gotten in the room when Julie began turning up the heat. Now that the context was different, she explained, she hoped this project would offer "a chance for me to turn over a new leaf at the company." Normally that kind of statement would have been sufficient bait for me to go into attack mode. (You can see now, can't you, why the visualization and practice exercises are so essential? If you haven't taken time to bring yourself into alignment with your new approach, it's easy to snap back into old, negative habits, and watch helplessly as things go downhill.)

What I did instead of becoming angry was to observe my own reactions, suspend and set aside my judgment, and try a new approach with Julie. While previously I would have resisted her at every opportunity, this time, when she made a suggestion that I thought was ill-informed or untenable, I asked, "OK. How might do we do that?"

My old firm had assigned Julie and me to deal with what we called "zombie accounts." These were accounts that were usually dead in the water, but that our salespeople nevertheless claimed were worth the time, effort, and expense to try and resurrect. One of the reasons Sales wanted us to try to revive these accounts was so that they could avoid cold-calling and breaking into new companies, which was not easy.

Most of these "zombies" had a stench of long-term decay about them, and I was skeptical about whether it was worth bothering to go down the list. Given that I wanted to work more effectively with Julie—who did think there was more money to be squeezed out of these accounts—I stopped myself from dismissing the possibility, even though I remained doubtful.

I continued to respond openly and respectfully to Julie's point of view. I remembered that my goal was as much about creating a positive, successful working relationship with her as it was about generating more money for the firm. If the relationship did not work, we would never make any more money for the firm, in any case.

I couldn't have been more surprised at how quickly Julie's demeanor changed—and how fundamentally. To our joint surprise, we both achieved a partial win. As we pursued these zombie accounts, Julie was able to see that my intuition—that there was considerably less money to be gained from them than she had thought—was right. But there were some benefits to reviewing these accounts that I had not realized. By looking at the accounts in detail, Julie and I were able to help the organization develop more accurate financial forecasts and better understand why they had lost the accounts to begin with.

Had I caused Julie to change? Not really. It was *my* being willing to change and taking practical steps to hold to that higher intention that made the real difference. By modifying my relationship strategy so that it was no longer a zero-sum game but a win-win, I had created a functional path down which we could walk together. This contrasted with the dysfunctional path we had each taken to get our individual needs met in the past. Our ongoing partnership was never perfectly smooth, of course, but working together became less fraught for both of us. Through this improved relationship, we were able to achieve a number of important breakthroughs that enhanced our reputation, both within the company and with each other.

At some point in your career, you have likely experienced a similar business relationship challenge and are wondering how you might learn to achieve your own breakthrough change—for yourself, your team, and your organization. That is what I'll be showing you throughout this book.

Where We're Going and How It Will Work

Drawing on my grandfather Kurt Lewin's legacy about how transformational change takes place, I have adapted his paradigm of unfreezing, reforming, and refreezing to organize the book into three sections that will allow you to quickly and permanently transform yourself and your relationships:

Part One: Unfreezing and New Awareness will provoke you to look afresh at the beliefs and assumptions that exist in your mind, and perhaps your organizational culture, which may be contributing to more breakdowns than breakthroughs. You learn the key attributes of resilient business relationships and will be prompted to ask questions of yourself and others in order to create a new awareness, reimagine what is possible, and make informed decisions about what you intend to achieve.

Part Two: Reforming and Making New Choices delves even further into the resilient business relationships model outlined in Part One. Here we spell out in greater detail what's involved in developing and maintaining relationships that are strong, flexible, and fair enough to thrive under challenge and not collapse into breakdown mode. A few key strategies, combined with the practical exercises and prompts found in these chapters, are designed to help you apply your new awareness and skills in order to experience quick, specific, beneficial results.

Part Three: Refreezing and Locking in Change offers advice and guidance on how to implement new values, behaviors, rewards, and metrics within your team, department, and division, and throughout your organization, so that resilient business relationships—internally and externally—become part of your culture and a source of sustained advantage.

As Scott Noteboom, the former Head of Infrastructure Strategy, Design & Development at Apple (essentially Cloud products and services)—one of a number of leading executives interviewed for this book who have shared their stories—has pointed out:

> "Whenever a big change occurs, the engineering mindset tends to go to 'I,' as in: 'what do *I* need to do?' Whereas a true leader who needs to get things done realizes that's not the right perspective. It has to be about community and aligning others with a vested interest in the envisioned outcome. *Our* solution is so much stronger than *my* solution. At the end of it you have a team that produces more, has more trust in each member and ends up better all around."

By the time you have read this book, worked through the exercises, and implemented the advice given, you will know:

- Why some relationships survive and get stronger under conditions of change and stress while others fail and break down.
- What characterizes resilient business relationships and how your most important relationships stack up.
- How you can build the key business relationships you need to succeed.
- How you can save those key business relationships that appear to be heading toward breakdown mode.
- How to ensure that your team, and perhaps the entire organization, can develop the resilient relationships needed for sustained success.

At this point, you will know how to operate confidently and permanently in breakthrough mode.

This book is not a course in basic communication skills, however. We are assuming that you already know how to have crucial conversations, share effective feedback, actively listen, and conduct successful meetings. (For further advice and guidance on those issues, you'll find a number of books and other resources listed in the Bibliography.)

Nor is it a book about large-scale organizational change methodologies or how to create effective teams. This book offers a practical model that explains how you can transform yourself using techniques that allow you to create effective business relationships, whether they be manager-employee, customer-supplier, or cross-functional. With these tools at your fingertips, you can enjoy the strong, flexible, and fair relationships that are the foundation of sustained and personally satisfying twenty-first century business success.

Are you ready to move forward? Then get yourself settled in and comfortable; just be sure to choose a reliable chair.

PART ONE
UNFREEZING AND NEW AWARENESS

Chapter One

THE POWER OF RESILIENT BUSINESS RELATIONSHIPS

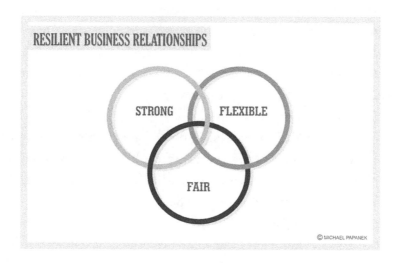

n the mid-1980s, I was a junior systems engineer working in Detroit for Electronic Data Systems (EDS). General Motors had just acquired the company, and I was part of a team hired to help what was seen as a slow and bureaucratic organization by dragging it into the twentieth century—before it was too late.

The GM/EDS merger was in big trouble even before I arrived in Michigan. Although the CEOs of both companies, Roger Smith and Ross Perot, were (at least according to the press releases) very excited about the "synergies" of the two companies, the employees were not so thrilled. Experienced GMers who had created and worked on various systems for years were forced to work with new and inexperienced EDS employees, who dressed and acted very differently. EDS recruited "eagles" and only "the best of the best." Along with many other young and overconfident EDS employees at the time, I tended to look down on our GM counterparts, believing that if they had been any good at their jobs they would not have needed us to step in.

This ultracompetitive environment caused each group of employees to assume that the other side did not appreciate them or share their goals or values. Worse still, each group felt they had to protect themselves and attack the other side in order to not lose power. Relationships within the new company were largely in breakdown mode.

Do you recognize this scenario?

One part of the onboarding process for new hires like myself was to send us to get work signed off on by a GM employee I'll call "Mr. No." He never approved anything, and was notorious for criticizing results, changing requirements, and erecting barriers to all things EDS. Apparently, he had decided that the only way to be loyal to his GM teammates was to do everything he could to ensure the merger failed. Meeting with him had become a rite of passage for the new guys.

To this day I still remember that ride up in the elevator, holding the first document I'd been given for his sign-off. All I really wanted was to get out alive, with my head and my dignity intact. But the first time I met with Mr. No, he lived up to his reputation, sending me packing with the words, "I will never approve anything you bring me, so stop trying!"

Yet there I was, the next day, trying again. My plan was simply to ask him enough times (and get enough "no's") to justify going around him. The commonly used strategy was to arrive armed for a fight; of course, we then got what we expected.

Although it wasn't a deliberate or conscious strategy on my part, I decided to set aside the assumptions of my peers, some of whom who saw Mr. No as a tired, retired-in-place, "vesting and resting" bureaucrat who added little to no value. Standing in his office one day, I happened to notice he had some family pictures on his desk, including some of two boys in hockey uniforms. So I began asking him about his kids.

At first I could see that he was suspicious of my motives: was this some kind of trick to get him to agree to sign off? But since I knew a little bit about hockey and was genuinely interested in the game, I continued questioning him about his sons: what position they played, were they planning to play in college, and so forth. Then I turned to leave. This was "Mr. No," after all, and I wasn't expecting miracles. But he called me back, asked to see the document again, then went ahead and signed on the dotted line.

My colleagues were shocked. I had treated this man as a human being and showed sincere interest in what interested him, and—guess what—he responded in kind. Over a period of several months, Mr. No and I became closer. Working together, we served as a channel for communication between the GM and EDS groups, especially when contentious issues needed to be discussed openly and resolved quickly.

After seeing how successful Mr. No and I became once we changed our approach, others began doing something similar. This created a butterfly effect[7] that shifted not just individual relationships but entire

---

7   The "Butterfly Effect" is the idea that in a complex system small changes can have large impacts. For instance, a butterfly's wings in Brazil could help create a tornado in Kansas.

teams and organizations. These strengthened relationships helped to build real value for the organization and allowed employees to implement more innovative changes.

In short, despite the stressful conditions we were all under, we helped to transition the teams from breakdown to breakthrough.

Riding the Heat Curve

Before I outline the three key factors characterizing resilient business relationships, let me address why this is so important to you. It all has to do with what I call your ability to "ride the heat curve."

It's the classic conundrum: we need a certain amount of stress and challenge to inspire creativity and innovation, and to motivate us to take action. The light gray line on the heat curve map (Figure 1, below) represents the optimal conditions for breakthroughs to occur. But there comes a point at which the curve begins a downward spiral, leading to breakdown. This is the point at which the "heat"—in the form of creative tension, interpersonal conflict, or extreme emotion—becomes too much for the individual or team to handle.

Figure 1:

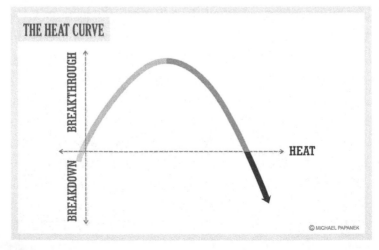

Unfortunately many leaders fail to see or understand this dynamic in action, let alone manage it well. Some make the mistake of reducing the heat too early in the process, often because they fear the situation will spiral out of control. Most leaders act this way because they don't understand how, by first developing resilient relationships, a leader can allow the rising curve of breakthrough to be sustained far beyond what could normally be achieved.

That, then, is the primary advantage of creating resilient relationships: the more resilience you have, the higher you are able to ride the heat curve and leverage the benefits of increasing stress—without the costs.

Let's take a look at this from another angle: conducting meetings.

"Nice" Meetings

Most commonly experienced in academia, state agencies, and nonprofits, but also many businesses, the "nice" meeting goes something like this:

There is an agenda and everyone follows it to the letter. There are no raised voices, and each person speaks knowing he or she will be given all the time they need to be heard. There is no conflict or controversy, and everyone acts respectfully. Should anyone be foolish enough to touch upon anything remotely controversial, they soon get the message from the group to back off.

Although there is no "heat" and certainly no pain during these kinds of meetings, this level of comfort also means that issues are rarely, if ever, resolved. Little or no creativity or innovation occurs, there's precious little risk-taking or leadership, and stronger relationships based on mutual trust typically don't get built. Any real concerns or radical ideas that may have existed are kept underground to fester unresolved and unaddressed. For the participants, the entire meeting is flat, boring, and lacking in value. The experience does not reflect reality, because reality is rarely "nice."

Breakdown Meetings

Contrast that with those meetings where there's too much "heat." In these kinds of meetings, the desire may be to ensure that everything is "out on the table" in a full and frank manner, but all too often these breakdown meetings devolve into "blame-storming" and pointing fingers. Anger replaces empathy, people begin talking past each other, feelings get hurt, and any remotely good intentions soon fly out the window.

The interactions that occur in these meetings are fueled by plenty of passion, but the excessive heat—when unaccompanied by the salve of resilience—means that too many people, ideas, and relationships get burned. Everyone feels worse off at the end than when they started, and the situation is far too volatile for meaningful collaboration to survive, let alone thrive.

Breakthrough Meetings

What we're always hoping to experience, and what this book will help you create, are those breakthrough meetings where no one checks out. Why? Because it's too important and too exciting to do anything other than pay attention and participate fully. Some people may have a tendency to talk at once; voices may be raised in excitement or even anger. But everyone knows that this is a consequence of talking about *real* issues, making tough decisions and firm choices, resolving differences, and moving forward passionately. Participants leave these meetings feeling energized and eager to share what happened with their team, and have a renewed strength and commitment not only to the plan but also to one another.

When was the last time you experienced a meeting like that? Rare, aren't they? That's because insufficient focus is placed on building resilient relationships in the first place.

You Do Not Have a "Relationship Type"

Just like each meeting, each relationship has its own heat curve. Some are enhanced by change, stress, and heat, while others are diminished by tension and disagreement. A significant failing with most tools that purport to assess a leader's abilities in the areas related to the heat curve (trust, conflict, communication skills, aggressiveness, openness) is that they assume each of us has a single "relationship type." However, most of us know from experience that some of our relationships can handle little or no heat at all, while others can survive and even thrive under massive change or stress. Relationships represent a dynamic, so thinking in terms of one person's skills and behavior makes no sense at all.

You are not a "D" (DISC) or a "Yellow" (Colors) or an "INTJ" (Myers-Briggs) or a "7" (Enneagram) in every situation. We all have different heat curves and they depend on two key factors: 1) The context or environment in which the relationship occurs; and 2) The nature of the existing relationship and whether it is strong, flexible, and fair.

Our relationship resilience depends on both context (what is happening that affects the relationship) and our current relationships (how we are connected today). Some environments or contexts encourage resilience; others inhibit it. In *The Geography of Thought*, author Richard Nisbett looks at the impact that different countries' cultures have on relationships and how moving from one country to another can dramatically change how much "heat" is acceptable before someone goes into breakdown mode. That is why you can so easily make a faux pas and accidentally create heat abroad with an offhand comment or action that would not be an issue "back home."

You Can't Listen Your Way Out of This

We'll revisit the heat curve throughout this book as a way of visually representing the kinds of business interactions we are increasingly experiencing in today's VUCA world. Let me just stress one further point.

You may be wondering where the concept of "soft skills" fits into all this. You might be asking yourself if it wouldn't be beneficial to enroll yourself or your people in training courses aimed at developing better listening skills, or to receive coaching on how to have "tough" conversations.

That is a seductive possible solution, certainly—except that the learning is unlikely to stick when the going gets tough. Soft skills do matter, just not enough to help you effectively handle a steeper heat curve. While generous listening, good facilitation, and other communication approaches make a difference, if the underlying *structure* of your relationships is unsound, communication skills will always fall short. As the maxim goes: actions speak louder than words.

For a relationship to be truly resilient and thrive—not merely survive—under pressure and change, good communication skills are insufficient. What you need are relationships with the following three key attributes: strong, flexible, and fair.

The Resilient Business Relationship

Strong: The relationship must produce value that contributes to the strategic goals that each person cares about, with the total value created (the relationship *purpose*) exceeding the effort each person puts into the relationship.

You know you have a strong relationship if it provides value that is hard to replace, would be missed if it were lost, and meets the critical goals of each party. Weak relationships are superficial and provide only marginal value, are easily replaced, and can pretty much be lived without. In order to provide real value, each party must have a certain level of intimacy or closeness that allows them to share what they really need and want out of the relationship. This is typically regarded as an undesirable vulnerability in many organizations, but it is essential for relationships built on resilient bedrock, rather than the shifting sands of superficial goals.

Strong relationships are based on a deep understanding of the other party. Who are they, where did they come from, what are their skills and experience, and why are their goals important to them?

For example, many years ago, during the time I was at EDS, I attended a very basic management course that could be summed up with the acronym KYP: Know Your People. This advice still makes sense today. Superficial knowledge and understanding leads to superficial outcomes and tenuous relationships. When we really know and understand each other as people, we can build strong, honest, and resilient relationships.

When I first got to GM, we were in some ways providing negative value because our actions went against so many of the stakeholders' interests. We had to *earn* respect, sometimes through the brute force of many hours, before we could even begin to address strategic issues. Communication was not going to happen until we produced the results the GM people valued. We were stuck in a classic "chicken-and-the-egg" situation: we could not produce results because we had poor relationships, and we could not build good relationships because of our weak results. We needed a breakthrough, a way out of this vicious cycle. By focusing less on results early on (even though we were under massive pressure to produce them), and by taking the time to connect as *people*, we created the breakthrough that shifted the relationship and put us on a more virtuous path.

> *"We have major work to do [reinventing PayPal] and this will not happen if people focus just on business and not on building strong, resilient relationships. Establishing a relationship is a commitment to being open, listening and working together*

towards a common goal and making it safe so that you can agree to disagree and build trust."
 —**Christine Landon**, former director, eBay/PayPal

Flexible: Relationships that stand the test of time are able to flex when situations change; they can still function and create the intended value. A resilient bridge is strong enough to carry traffic, yet flexible enough to withstand high winds or earthquakes. Flexibility in the human dynamic means sharing power, allowing yourself to be influenced by another's input, and being prepared to build *shared* solutions.

If you want to influence others, you must first be willing to be influenced yourself. Flexibility in relationships means showing respect for the changing needs of others by adapting and modifying the relationship based on everyone's needs, not just your own. If only one person or group is absorbing all the impact of a change, invariably they will look for new ways to gain value and may end up abandoning the relationship altogether if they don't find it. For resilient business relationships, we need to be flexible about our own needs as things change, while respecting that others have needs that are important to them.

At EDS, our strategy had been to remain rigid and strong, focus on our own needs, and escalate issues once we reached conflict, which became known as "bringing in the big guns" and "getting all the liars in one room." This inflexibility merely pushed people deeper into their already entrenched positions ("I will not sign anything!"), even if it meant failing to make progress toward our own best interests. By focusing on the battle, we lost our ability to see other options. Flexibility does not have to mean giving up your needs, however. In the end, Mr. No and I both got what we wanted (good quality code that was tested and put into production). We just had to be flexible about how we got there.

In a study by IBM entitled "Leading Through Connections,"[8] the CEOs polled said they are now changing the profile of what they want from top leaders. While expertise and business or technical knowledge remain valuable, the ability to team across the C-suite and create collaborative environments were two of the top attributes valued by CEOs, with 58 percent stating that "teaming" was a critical leadership trait. The study reported:

> "As CEOs ratchet up the level of openness within their organizations, they are developing collaborative environments where employees are encouraged to speak up, exercise personal initiative, connect with fellow collaborators, and innovate."

Fair: Unlike bridges, human beings need more than strength and flexibility. Relationships that have both of these characteristics can still break down under stressful conditions if the value created within that dynamic is not perceived as honestly and equitably shared.

In this regard, it is the intention for the relationship (as it was during my experience with Julie) that is the most important consideration. Is the goal of all parties to support and enhance each other, or is it to compete and "win" at the expense of the other side losing? Are all parties willing to openly share their real goals and intentions?

This is perhaps a more complex factor to understand than being strong and flexible. There is no cookie-cutter approach to what different people in a relationship consider to be "fair." In this context, "fair" does not mean "equal."

For example, back in the 1990s, when I was a partner at a small consulting firm in San Francisco, there was a major focus on compensation and fairness. During one of our many conversations

---

8   IBM Institute for Business Value, "Leading Through Connections," 2012 IBM CEO Study, May 2012.

about this issue, a young man who had been with the firm for about a year suggested we take all our profits (any revenue above costs) and divide that equally among all employees: to him that would be fair, meaning equal gain. To me, however, fair meant equitable distribution of gains based on contribution. Is one party giving more but not receiving a commensurate share of the gains? We were a team, certainly, but some of us had worked for years to create the company this young man was now a part of, and we had developed the actual products and services, competed in a crowded marketplace, and spent years developing our skills. When I asked him, "Would you like to earn the same you are making today after twenty years in this business?" he started to see that equal would be very unfair in this case. So, fair often has more to do with who is giving and who is getting, and how much.

The other key issue of fairness is trust. To what extent do you feel confident about handing over some or all of your power to the other party? If you really trust someone, such that you would go to hell and back together and come out relatively unscathed, with the relationship intact, you feel safe about giving up total power over something that's important to you.

Because of some poor results at the start of the GM/EDS merger, mentioned earlier, many people at GM did not believe they could trust and share power with the new EDS employees. This was not unreasonable from the GM line managers' point of view. After all, why should they be expected to share in the accountability for results with people they neither knew well nor trusted? Mr. No, for example, felt he was being asked to willingly accept equal blame if things went wrong by being asked to say "yes" to data he did not trust and that might unfairly put his excellent reputation on the line. Worse still, when things went well, the EDS group tended to hog the credit, but wanted to blame the GM people when things did not work—an unfair sharing of credit and blame. When I started admitting to our challenges and mistakes, and built a record of keeping my promises, Mr. No began to see that I had things I was accountable for, and that his blind obstruction was also not being fair to me.

Bottom-Line Benefits

Interaction Associates has been studying the link between trust, relationships, and financial results since 2009. In *Building Trust in Business 2015: How Top Companies Leverage Trust, Leadership and Collaboration*, they reported that organizations with high levels of trust, honesty, and fairness had consistently higher financial results, were better at employee retention, and had employees with more confidence in the organization's ability to weather an economic crisis:

- Highly collaborative companies were significantly more productive, entrepreneurial, and innovative than other companies (74 percent of highly collaborative companies versus 22 percent of others).
- 62 percent of high-performing organizations reported that effective leadership and collaboration—and high levels of trust—help retain key employees, compared with only 30 percent of low-performing organizations.
- Treating employees fairly, no matter their rank or position, is a strongly exhibited behavior inside high-performing organizations and is 11 percent more prevalent than in low-performing organizations.

Two Out of Three Is Not Enough
Fair and Flexible but Not Strong = Superficial

When the relationship is fair and flexible but is not strong (does not produce important value for the parties), it is superficial and easily replaced. It's "nice," but not important enough to be resilient. This is the vendor we call only when our first choice is not available, or it's the job we take until we find something better.

Strong and Fair but Not Flexible = Tenuous

When the business relationship produces important outcomes and is fair to both parties but is not flexible, it is tenuous and may fall apart under changing conditions. For example, when organizations become too rigid, they may lose customers as soon as a competitor can match their value and is more open to customer needs. This may have been the case at Cisco and Apple: each became dominant in their markets by providing value, but have lost share to organizations that follow more flexible policies. These relationships are often described with statements like "great product and fair price, but what a hassle to deal with."

Strong and Flexible but Not Fair = Coercive

A relationship that produces outcomes and can adapt to change but is not fair is coercive. This is often the case when there are few available options, such as when there is one large employer in a remote geographic area who then takes dvantage of and exploits the lack of options for its employees, or when there are too few competitors in a given market and so customer service suffers, such as in the cable TV industry of the 1990s.

Food for Thought

We all work with many competent employees, vendors, partners, and clients who meet expectations and create value. But many of these relationships tend to come and go in a rapidly changing business world. The relationships that stand the test of time are strong, flexible, and fair, even when the unexpected happens.

In Section Two of this book, you will learn a practical process for evaluating and improving your most important business relationships.

In the meantime, I encourage you to review the following questions so you can immediately embed the learning from this chapter. It might be helpful if, instead of answering them in relation to your business relationships generally, you focus on one relationship you care about that is at risk of breaking down:

Is This Relationship Strong?

- To what extent is the value created by this relationship synergistic, meaning that by working together you produce a greater result than even combining the individual value you bring to the table?
- If this relationship were to disintegrate tomorrow, how easily could you replace it with another? What would you miss the most about it?
- How frequently (if ever) do you discuss what you want and need out of your relationship with the other party?
- How well do you really know and understand each other as individuals in this relationship, over and above your job titles and roles?
- What have you done recently to connect in ways that move beyond discussing process and results?

Is This Relationship Flexible?

- When conditions change and you are asked for something new or more from this relationship, how do you tend to react?
- How open are you to being influenced by the opinions and needs of the other party?
- When was the last time you had a discussion about upcoming challenges and what you might need to do to head them off before a conflict occurs?

- On a scale of one to ten, how collaborative do you consider this relationship to be? Would your partners be likely to give this relationship the same or a similar rating?

Is This Relationship Fair?

- Who benefits most from the value you add to this relationship? Do you create value mostly for your own gain, or are the gains fairly distributed (and would the other party be likely to think the same as you do)?
- If one party had the ability to end the relationship, would they be likely to do so—and for what reason(s)?
- How much do you trust this partner—and do they really trust you?
- What is your ultimate goal or intention here: to do what is right for both sides, or to compete with your partner such that you are most likely to win regardless of the cost to them?

In this chapter, we have explored the nature of resilient relationships with respect to the way they contribute toward riding the heat curve. Shifting the heat curve of the relationship leads to greater chances of creative and innovative interactions because we can advance together at a higher, steeper level than might otherwise be possible. Plus we have examined the three factors—strong, flexible, and fair—that characterize such relationships.

Before we move on to a process you can use to ensure that all your important business relationships are resilient, we need to look at how change *really* happens. Because it's not the way people usually think it does.

Chapter Two

HOW CHANGE HAPPENS

S
cott Noteboom had a reputation as a hard hitter, for more reasons than one. Previously with Yahoo!, where he was responsible for global network operations, Scott was your archetypal engineer, the kind of individual that Art Kleiner—in a *Strategy + Business* article titled "The Cult of Three Cultures"— described as being "stimulated by puzzles and problems, and by the design challenge of creating an ideal world of elegant machines that operate in harmony." Quoting MIT culture expert Edgar Schein, whose three-culture theory (representing the operational, executive, and engineering parts of a business) was the topic in question, Kleiner's article went on to point out that the focus for engineers is "designing humans *out* of the systems rather than into them."[9]

---

9   Art Kleiner. "The Cult of Three Cultures." *Strategy + Business*, July 1, 2001.
     http://www.strategy-business.com/article/19868?gko=04205

Certainly Scott was not a man known for a great deal of interpersonal finesse. He approached his work somewhat similarly to the way he approached his hobby, boxing: protect yourself and your team, attack anyone who gets in your way, and play to win through overwhelming power and force. This approach worked for Scott throughout his career as he rose rapidly from engineer to director, producing knockout results every time. Unfortunately, the trail was often littered with people unable to stand up to such an onslaught.

Here was a man who could be ruthlessly dedicated to getting his way, at any cost. If you had asked Scott some years back how he'd achieved success, his language would have been peppered with phrases like "going for the knockout," being "bulletproof" in meetings, and "shooting down" opposing points of view. He cared deeply about people and, for those who could stay with him under the heat of his intensity and drive, he would do anything for them. It was a tough team that accomplished great results, day after day. But Scott's "heat curve" was too intense for many people, and they either self-selected out of his team or were removed by Scott.

As Scott rose higher in his company's hierarchy (he left Yahoo! to become a senior vice president at Apple, where he led the Cloud products and services division, and is now the CEO of a start-up), he began to notice that the competitive boxer energy that had propelled his success as an individual performer was hampering his ability to cement the team relationships he now relied upon. The higher he went in the organization, the more he had to learn to lead through *influence* rather than sheer brute force of will.

In the past, Scott's role had been more about execution of other people's strategies, and as long as that worked, he tended to be left alone by his managers to run things his way. I met Scott just as he was moving into a more senior role, which required not just innovative, industry-leading technical strategies and solutions, but also buy-in and support from other executive members of his team. These people did not work for him and had the power to accept, resist, or actively support his ideas. Scott was dependent on them to reach his goals and vision. The context had changed!

At Apple, Scott had an example of a leader: the legendary Steve Jobs, whose own relationship brand was similarly demanding, critical, harsh, even brutal, yet at the same time highly successful.

What Scott began to notice was that his emphasis on being "the smartest guy in the room" was fostering considerable dysfunction within and among teams as they competed against each other in a win-lose, rather than collaborative, model of leadership. If you're skeptical as to whether this approach has an impact on the bottom line, consider Microsoft. In a *Vanity Fair* article[10] pointing to Steve Ballmer's similarly combative style of leadership, author Kurt Eichenwald reported that the company's market capitalization stood at $510 billion in December 2000 but had dropped to $249 billion by the middle of 2012.

Writing about the culture of Microsoft at the dawn of the millennium, Eichenwald pointed out that:

"In those years Microsoft had stepped up its efforts to cripple competitors, but—because of a series of astonishingly foolish management decisions—the competitors being crippled were often co-workers at Microsoft, instead of other companies. Staffers were rewarded not just for doing well but for making sure that their colleagues failed. As a result, the company was consumed by an endless series of internal knife fights. Potential market-busting businesses—such as e-book and smartphone technology—were killed, derailed, or delayed amid bickering and power plays."

---

10   Kurt Eichenwald, "Microsoft's Lost Decade," *Vanity Fair*, August 2012. http://www.vanityfair.com/news/business/2012/08/microsoft-lost-mojo-steve-ballmer

As Scott now sees it, "Some leaders can play that game and meddle with people's emotions and get a stronger product. Externally that might be an effective way to compete, but internally it's extremely damaging."

It was not just the other executives who put pressure on Scott to improve his business relationships, but his team members as well. In Silicon Valley, indeed in any of today's growth industries, the very best people tend to have the most options. Keeping team members engaged, motivated, and productive is key to staying competitive in the ongoing, escalating war for talent. In the past, there had been enough people with the right skills to ensure that Scott could quickly replace lost talent. Now the work was even more complex and he could not afford to have any unintended turnover. For Scott, the heat generated by this particular curve was starting to singe his heels.

How could someone as strong and driven as Scott change to better meet the challenges with which he was now tasked? How might he engender commitment rather than fear within his direct reports and strengthen his relationships with other senior executives? He needed to develop relationships that were resilient and capable of producing breakthroughs rather than breaking down under stress.

Many organizations take a Nike approach to change, saying "just do it" and expecting that everyone involved will embrace new attitudes, behaviors, and values overnight. Maybe you have experienced this yourself. Perhaps you received feedback during a 360-degree program or performance appraisal when you were told there was an issue with the way you dominated others in meetings and that you should listen more and let others speak. This may have made complete sense to you, and, wishing to become more of a team player, perhaps you decided to do just that—until the next meeting came around and you found yourself falling back into old habits.

Most of us are completely sincere when we accept negative feedback and maintain that we will change our ways as a consequence. So what goes wrong? Here's the problem: change is not an overnight accomplishment. Simply *deciding to change* doesn't mean that change will happen. The secret to real, sustained change is that it only follows *new awareness*.

What do I mean by that?

Back in the 1940s, Kurt Lewin, founding father of Organizational Development, used scientific methods to better understand social dynamics and created a three-phase model. Although the concept is well accepted, if not always practiced, the breakthrough idea at the time was that change is a *process*, not an event. First you had to prepare to change (which Lewin referred to as "Unfreezing"), then you had to change your thinking and start testing new ideas ("Forming"), and finally you sustained that change by embedding new behaviors ("Refreezing"). Thousands of leaders within organizations as diverse as Chevron, Bank of America, Charles Schwab, and Yahoo! use Lewin's approach to embed a new way of relating that could be sustained over time.

My version of Lewin's three-phase model looks like this:

1. First must come the *awareness* that self-change needs to occur because you are looking to produce different outcomes.
2. Then comes determination and understanding, critically examining your existing choices in order to make new ones; you must *choose* to do something different.
3. Finally comes the implementation phase as a period of *change* to see what happens and the extent to which new, improved outcomes result. This third, experimental phase is critical to providing the evidence you need to fully embrace the new attitudes and behaviors that will bring about desired outcomes.

What commonly happens after we receive negative feedback? We want to take immediate action to change things for the better and experience speedy results. So we zip through the awareness part, make a quick choice to stop doing whatever was causing the problem in the first place, and then believe we have changed.

As I pointed out earlier, that may produce some temporary new results, but to achieve long-term, meaningful change requires a lot more emphasis and time at the front end.

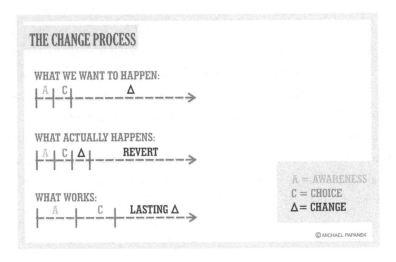

This strategy of deeper awareness, choice-making, and testing in order to lock in new behaviors scales to the individual, team, and organizational levels. And we are not talking years or even months to see beneficial results. In Scott's case, the process began to pay off in a matter of weeks.

Here's how it played out in Scott's experience, as he realized that to continue to serve his organization as superbly as he always had, he would need to take off his boxing gloves and shift to a more flexible, mutual, and relationship-oriented approach.

Awareness

The first step for Scott was to select an outcome that he was truly concerned about and needed to change. We identified an upcoming meeting where Scott was to present an important proposal for an idea that he and his team had been working on for some time. The participants at this meeting would either give their approval (and an extensive budget) to proceed with his idea, or not. Scott already had some concerns about achieving that outcome and felt this was as good an opportunity as any to try some new and more effective strategies.

Acting as Scott's coach, I asked him about his concerns and to outline for me the plans he had for reaching a successful conclusion at this meeting. He knew that a number of people would be threatened by this idea, given that it required other teams to change how they did business. It would also draw a certain amount of budget away from them to him, despite helping the business overall. Scott expected considerable resistance from those who would feel most threatened, which could negatively influence the senior executive who had to make the final decision and was known to dislike overruling his management team because he valued consensus. Scott's current plan was to create an overwhelming, irrefutable business case, so the naysayers would have to back down. He told me he knew there would be bullets flying, but was convinced that he was bulletproof. This sounded to me like the same old Scott: that the boxing gloves had appeared again.

We examined more deeply *why* Scott thought this approach would work. For one thing, Scott told me, this strategy had always worked well in the past with his team members and prior manager, and secondly, all that mattered to him was the "right" answer, based on the "right" data, which he always worked very hard to find. The trouble was, now Scott was operating in a different environment, one among equals over whom he had no direct authority. Was it likely that this well-used strategy would work in a different context?

I asked Scott to take the next week and observe himself in meetings, to notice when he found himself using this dominating approach, and to ask himself some questions: why am I doing this now? What do I want? What is actually happening? What do I see, hear, or feel from the others in the room? Am I achieving what I want to happen? I asked him not to form a judgment (good or bad) about what he observed, just to make notes and wait for insights to emerge rather than try to force them. His focus needed to be on those situations where his actions led to what he wanted, as well as those that resulted in unintended negative consequences.

When we spoke a week later, Scott's new sense of awareness had produced considerable data to work with. He told me he tended to use his more dominating style whenever he felt his ideas were under attack. He would feel frustrated that valuable time was being used up when "we were just going to end up doing it my way anyway." He also noticed that this reaction tended to shut down questions from others in the group. In one-on-one meetings, Scott discovered he was less likely to consider questions as "problems" or challenges to his thinking. That was a huge insight that provided a framework for how he would proceed.

Choice

Scott recognized that while he felt that his domineering approach was a way to give his team members clear direction, it did not allow for much give-and-take. Because he did not have ultimate power in this new scenario, he needed more than compliance for this upcoming meeting. Scott could deduce from those weeklong self-awareness exercises that some of his dominating behavior was resulting in outcomes he did not want—such as the lack of ownership of his ideas by others. He also realized that his old behavior was unlikely to work in his new role.

Following that awareness, Scott made a new choice—still based on deeply held goals and values—that to succeed in the upcoming meeting he needed to achieve alignment and agreement, not win a battle. He was willing to try something new to *get* something new. Scott chose to value the support of others more than he had before, when he was focused only on what the data said and how the problem could be solved. Scott was committed to blending his strength with a more flexible and fair approach.

Only now was Scott ready to implement true change. He had a strategy and a goal, both of which he owned. He continued to observe his behavior without trying to change it. We continued to look at what new ideas he could test to see if they would benefit him during the critical upcoming meeting.

Change

As the date of the meeting drew near, we looked for opportunities to try out some new approaches based on the outcomes Scott wanted.

He set up one-on-one meetings with each key member of the management team to discuss his idea in advance and to share a "draft" for their input. Scott disclosed to me beforehand that his intention was one of collaboration and shared ownership. He asked the other participants in the forthcoming meeting not just to discuss the viability of his proposed idea, but also to suggest ways to work together effectively going forward. Once he had done everything he could to prepare for the meeting, Scott accepted that there was a chance he might not get the agreement he wanted, since by definition all change is unpredictable. As Yogi Berra once said, "It's hard to make predictions, especially about the future."

Scott took each person's input and concerns and used them to modify his proposal prior to the meeting. This made the proposal the team's idea and not just his. By the time the big meeting came along, the proposal was already mostly agreed to, and reaching alignment to move forward became easy and positive. No one was left behind, no punches were thrown, and no bullets flew.

So what key insights did Scott take away from his change process? He summed it up this way:

"'Our' solution proved to be so much stronger and more satisfying than 'my' solution. In my team I now notice that everyone seems a whole lot happier and performs a lot better. At the end you not only get more results, you get a team that produces more, has more trust in each other, and you end up getting more respect as well."

Scott was able to see these same factors at play in many other areas of his work: in team meetings and with vendors, partners, peers, and senior managers. He turned his reactive approach into one of choices: what method or behavior should I use now to achieve the results we need? Sometimes he needed to dial up the intensity; at other times he could moderate and listen more. What once was a "switch"—on or off—became a "dial" that he could turn at will. With this successful experience behind him, Scott could now replicate that strategy whenever he was faced with similar issues and goals.

Let's be very clear about one thing. Scott did not "lose" his essential self—he simply learned to become more aware of the impact of his actions and adjust them as and when needed. Rather than becoming less, he became more! He is still an intense individual because that is the source of his passion, drive, and inspiration to others. It's just that he is now a more effective leader with a broader range of responses, ones that continue to nurture key business relationships that are resilient to any major challenge.

Hopefully this kind of positive adaptation to unknown and highly stressful situations is attractive to you, because in the next chapter we are going to focus on how you can use this approach to discover just how resilient your most important current relationships are. We will then begin crafting the means by which relationships at risk of breakdown can be transformed into one breakthrough result after another.

Chapter Three
GETTING TO WHY

om Wolfe described the very wealthy Wall Street executive and main character in his novel *Bonfire of the Vanities* as a "Master of the Universe." My client, Bill, was a real-life version. A senior executive of a very prominent and highly specialized global investment firm, and the firm's top producer, Bill was, needless to say, very wealthy, extremely successful, and as tough as nails. He definitely played to win. Everything seemed perfect in a life filled with first-class business trips to Europe, club memberships, and industry accolades. But it wasn't.

A problem Bill had had for a long time finally caught up with him. Over his years at the firm, most in-house staffers who had anything to do with Bill either asked to be moved to another department, complained to HR, or quit. Finally, despite his consistent and "masterful" numbers, the CEO, a longtime friend, brought him in for a chat. The VP of HR quickly followed up. Bill was to get coaching for his obvious "people" issues, whether he wanted it or not.

Unlike Scott (mentioned in the last chapter), Bill had no inkling that he needed to change. More than that, he didn't want to. His response to both the CEO and the VP of HR was that the complainants obviously didn't understand the high-pressure nature of this business. Bill was a "producer" and didn't have time for all those "niceties." His response to the request to change was unequivocal: "These people need to get used to me or move on. I am great at what I do, and my style will *never* change. I care about *results*."

As the graph below indicates, up to this point Bill did not have the awareness necessary to begin to change on his own.

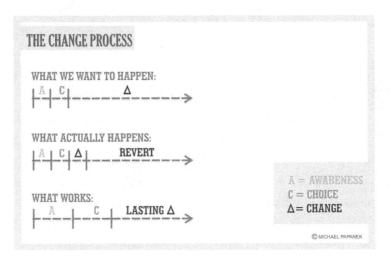

The Higher You Go, the More Relationships Matter
Just like Bill, many otherwise successful leaders have trouble with "the people side" of business. Team members, individual performers, and even many first-line supervisors are rewarded based on individual results that depend mostly on technical and operational skills. Many managers, therefore, may never have had to look very closely at their people-oriented abilities, so when they are promoted into more senior

positions, they are often lacking in the social intelligence and self-awareness needed in those roles.

Author and management consultant David Rock has written about how the importance of social skills and self-awareness rises relative to the importance of business and technical skills as one moves higher in an organization. In his 2013 *Fortune* magazine article "Why Organizations Fail,"[11] Rock reported that when sixty thousand managers across four continents were asked how many managers they thought could be placed in the top third of performers in terms of both of these areas—successfully achieving business goals *and* meeting the needs of other people—the respondents placed only a dismal 0.77 percent in that group. In their 2015 study "The State of the American Manager," Gallup found that only 10 percent of managers possessed the five key attributes needed to be a successful manager.[12]

All of which could be very good news for you, because it offers an opportunity to stand out from others in a way that is much needed in leadership today. You will be pretty special if you have sales, marketing, technical, or financial acumen and can also demonstrate and model the self-awareness and people skills that seem to be in such short supply.

Unfortunately, Bill, rather than seeing this situation as an opportunity to be masterful in a new area, took a great deal of persuading and cajoling to see that creating and closing very large financial deals was *not* all that mattered to his firm. As all those who knew him could attest, Bill's relationships mostly fell into the "coercive" category: while they were strong, they were certainly not flexible (with Bill, it was "my way or the highway"), or fair ("my needs matter, yours do not").

---

11   David Rock, "Why Organizations Fail," Fortune Magazine, October 23, 2013, http://fortune.com/2013/10/23/why-organizations-fail/

12   The five attributes were: motivating their employees, overcoming obstacles, creating a culture of accountability, building trusting relationships and making informed, unbiased decisions . "The State of the American Manager," 2015, Gallup. http://www.gallup.com/services/182138/state-american-manager.aspx

A Rare Brand of Leader

Bill had been lucky over the years, but the environment was changing and he wasn't flexible enough to do what was needed to meet the new realities. As the CEO and VP of HR recognized, but Bill did not, the greater heat of a volatile market and escalating global financial downturn was resulting in higher levels of stress throughout the firm. Internal collaboration, they knew, would be key to riding this out. Everyone needed to draw on their reserves of mutual support and loyalty, so they could not let Bill continue down his current path, given his poor history of internal relationship-building. Bill's resilience under change was being tested.

Bill's lack of awareness is in stark contrast to that of Christine Landon, who has built a long, successful career in Leadership Development and Human Resources in some of the top organizations in the world (HP, Agilent, eBay/PayPal and she has recently moved to Workday) by being one of the ".77 percent" with great skills in both areas.

Having operated in conditions of stress and change, Christine has seen how much relationships matter, especially in growing, high-performance cultures. Pushing for results by only using leverage and power to overcome obstacles is a losing strategy over the long term, she told me. When new people come in with a new role, or when you are the person who is asked to lead change, your focus cannot be about working *through* people but working *with* them. Rather than being a reason to ignore the "people side," as the pressure to perform increases so does the need for more effective relationships.

By using this relationship-oriented approach, Christine has become a key "connector" in Silicon Valley, well-known not only for her long-term and high quality relationships, but for helping others succeed. She has made the difference in so many people's careers over the years, by "collecting" the most talented people in the Valley, who now form a network that can address almost any need. This creates a level of security and positive power for her, and has led to a history of excellence that is a real asset in the very volatile Silicon Valley market.

As Christine says:

"When I came on board [at PayPal] I was told relationship-building is the most important thing that you have to do. I was given an onboarding plan and for the first few weeks I didn't really look at it because it had a list of 60 or 70 people I was expected to meet with while I had all these other business deliverables ... but then I realized that *I am not going to get any of this done if I don't know all these people*, develop connections, and listen deeply to understand the business challenges and opportunities leaders were facing across all functions and regions at PayPal. It also required me to Be the Customer and become a key user of our own products."

We have all met someone like Bill, and since you are reading this book, I assume you don't share his extreme views or behavior. Hopefully you have also met people like Christine, and aspire to be more like them. What you want to know is how to make that happen. What's the model or step-by-step guidance that will help you reach that rare position?

These are the kinds of questions I hear from my clients. And it's at this point that I have to tell them to hold their horses just a while longer, since it's not wise to dive into the "how" of something without first considering the "why."

In order to succeed with the material outlined in the rest of this book, you will first need to create a full-color, living, breathing picture of what success looks like for you, so you can maintain your momentum by drawing on reserves of positive motivation—especially when the going gets tough. To skip this step would be like rushing to build a house without bothering with a foundation: the first stiff breeze will blow it over.

Let me explain what I mean by expanding on that analogy.

Your Vision Is Your Motivation

I've experienced a number of times the greatest joy and horror of home ownership: the remodel. Anyone who has had major construction work done, whether you're upgrading a kitchen or ripping out an old bathroom, knows the pain: strangers in your house at all hours, no way to cook or store food, noise and dust, no running water, and a constant outflow of money to pay for it all.

On one occasion we underwent an extensive remodel of our home while I, my wife, our three young children, and five (yes five!) cats were living under the same roof. Our place was old, worn-out, and all the appliances were failing. We needed to make a change, and yet could not afford to move out for the six months that the work was estimated to take. We all know how accurate contractors are when it comes to both the time frame and the cost, right? I knew before we started that this was going to be a long, hard slog, the likes of which have ruined marriages before.

What kept me going was Thanksgiving. Not the actual experience of it, but maintaining a vision of the Thanksgiving holidays we would enjoy in our house of the future. This was my personal "why." Whenever I thought I would lose my mind, I summoned up a picture, almost a dream, of what the next Thanksgiving—after the remodel was over— would be like.

In my mind, I could smell the wonderful food being prepared. I could hear my wife telling me how much she loved cooking in a state-of-the-art chef's kitchen. There was now plenty of room, so for the first time we were able to invite all our relatives and some other families to join us, and I would see everyone having a great time.

When I was knee-deep in drywall, when the plumber woke me yet again at 7:00 am, when there was yet another modification to the time frame, I could look at the design elevations from the architect and I would fill them in my mind with real people having a great experience in the new space. When I signed yet another check, I could remember the reason why I was doing it all, and how much a positive difference it would make for me and my family.

Instead of metaphorically grabbing a hammer and starting to pound the nails in order to create change ASAP, "*Start With Why*," as the title of Simon Sinek's book urges. The process of change must be informed by strong, positive motivation, otherwise that change will fail when faced with the first real obstacle.

I found this to be especially true with Bill, who took some time to understand why he needed to change. Yet if we had not spent time on this vital piece of the process, reverting back to his established, comfortable habits would have be too easy—especially when the heat was turned up and a big deal was on the line.

Bill had never really thought about a vision for his relationships; his brand was all about having the highest numbers in the firm; nothing else mattered to him. But when we started to discuss that vision, and bring into focus what he wanted those relationships to be *like*, he began to create his own motivation to change. When others would tell him to change, it was always so he could meet *their* expectations. When he formed his *own* expectations, based on a more complete view of his values, he began the process needed for long-term change to be successful.

Bill's vision of being the top dog was already true, but what else mattered to Bill? What potential benefits was he leaving on the table? After conducting a 360-degree assessment of his interpersonal skills, Bill learned that his interactions with others caused them to feel diminished rather than enhanced. When Bill attacked, yelled at, and berated others, it got him what he wanted, but also made others feel less valued and disrespected. Despite all the complaints about his abrasiveness, and all the people leaving, this was a complete surprise to Bill. This just shows how effective the human mind can be at denying the reality of others (and we'll talk more about that in later chapters).

Building On Existing Values

I decided to first focus outside of Bill's work environment to find out more about his core values as a person. It turned out that my theory that the same people can have very different types of relationships (versus having only one dominant type) was correct. We identified a very important relationship he had outside of work—the one with his spouse—where he did not behave in the same dysfunctional way. We returned to the key question of why this relationship was different from his relationships at work. Bill's insight was that in the relationship with his spouse, respecting the value of human dignity was very important to him. He knew that his colleagues at the office had already said (through the 360-degree feedback) that human dignity was not a value he seemed to stand for with them. Certainly he was a tough guy in a tough industry, and he did not have one moment to waste on "being soft and fuzzy"—but just as he valued human dignity in his non-work life, he decided he wanted to live this in his professional life as well. Bill was willing to see whether collaboration based on loyalty and dedication—rather than compliance out of fear—would lead to better results for all concerned.

To flesh out his answer to the question of "why change?" Bill formed a new vision of what his relationships at the office would look like in the future:

From (Current State of Business Relationships)	To (Desired Future State)
I demand, you comply.	I listen, we agree.
I use my power and threats to make sure I get what I need.	I build agreements and share accountability for getting what I need.
How I treat you depends on your status, relative power, and role.	How I treat you is based on my enduring ethical values and principles, which do not change depending on the other person's position.
I am known as a tough, demanding, and difficult leader who gets results: "take me how I am."	I am known as a highly productive, passionate, and high-energy leader who is great to work with: "this is how I want to be remembered."

Bill wanted to build agreements, rather than use only power and authority to gain more commitment and buy-in from others. This would not only allow him to live out the value of human dignity; it turns out that this agreement-based approach also leads to more "discretionary effort," and better business returns, as outlined below by the consultants at Interaction Associates.

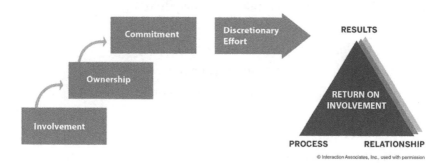

No one in this day and age—when collaboration, cooperation, and mutual benefit are high on the radar of most organizations—can go it alone. And the higher the stakes, the more you need others to manage the complexity with you. No one has all the skills or resources for every task they may be confronted with. More importantly, if you use power to get your own way, the chances are you might not be able to trust others to have your best interests in mind when there is a trade-off. The more complex the problem, the more social the solution needs to be. Successfully riding the heat curve is a *social* activity.

So, before we dive into the strategies and tools you will use to build more resilient relationships, you need to develop a robust picture of what the benefits will be *for you specifically* to make a real change in your relationships. Each day, you will have thousands of thoughts, make hundreds of decisions, and take scores of actions that over time will add up to your future. When you choose what you want that future to look like, you can sustain taking the actions to get you there. If you change only because others will benefit, you will have little motivation, much less passion, for making that change.

Even though he was under pressure from the CEO and head of HR, Bill made his own decision to prove to others that he values human dignity and that he acts based on ethical principles, not just for his own rewards. Bill recognized that this would help him to:

- Develop as a leader and a person
- Attract the best deals and best employees
- Build a more positive legacy over his last 10 years in the business

After four months of coaching, that is exactly what happened. Bill focused on each specific conversation or email interaction he had with his colleagues, and tried to make sure they reflected his new approach. He and I would debrief after each conversation, so that over time, through his own cycle of action and evaluation, Bill developed the skills he needed to create the new leadership brand he wanted. And do not worry, he is still kicking ass and taking names in the marketplace.

Build Your Own "From-To" Chart

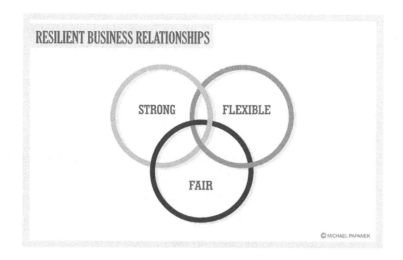

Before moving to the next chapter, you need to lock in your own motivation for building resilient relationships that are strong, flexible, and fair. Consider the following questions as you complete the worksheet below to form your own vision of why *you* would want to change:

1. **Who are your key relationships with?** We can easily miss acknowledging all the people who do so much for us and provide critical value. For example, one of the shocks of forming my solopreneur business was suddenly realizing that there was no marketing department to create my collateral, no legal department to write my contracts, no one "in accounting" to make sure I got paid or paid my bills, and on and on. At my age and level of experience I thought I had all I needed, but I did not. Make a list of all your most valuable relationships. These may include your partners, funders, clients, boss, peers, mentors, and any other functional support you receive.

2. **What is the current state and desired future for those key relationships?** Review from the perspective of the other person—practice the old adage to "walk a mile in their shoes" as you create a "from ... to" for each. Later we will undertake some exercises and have a relationship dialogue with the other person, but for now, simply ask yourself what these people would say if they were to be completely frank and honest about working with you.

3. **What are the values you would want to be reflected in your relationships?** Even if results and productivity are key, what else matters in your life? What would it look like for you to have the benefit of strong, flexible, and fair business relationships? What do you want to be known and remembered for? How do you want people to feel when they are working with you? What value do you want *them* to experience, beyond the value you receive from them? What descriptive words would you want someone to use if they were telling a story about working with you?

To give you an example, I have completed a sample row from the perspective of Bill as Sales VP, and his relationship with the VP of Marketing:

Person/ Group	From ...	To ...	Vision/Values/ Benefits: Strong-Flexible-Fair
VP Marketing (marketing group)	• I call them only when I need something. • I only give feedback when something is wrong. • I do not support all marketing programs and sometimes actively disparage their work with other VPs. • I am focused on my needs and what they can do for me.	• I provide help to them when they need it. • I give both positive and corrective feedback. • I make a good-faith effort (as determined by marketing) to implement new marketing programs. • We have two-way conversations which create the best solution for everyone.	• Mutual gain/ win-win. • Respect for others and their roles. • I am seen as a valued, albeit skeptical, partner. • I am a source of honest and actionable feedback. • I model the ideal relationship for other Sales VPs to follow. • I get more flexibility and faster responses from marketing. • I increase sales and shorten sales cycles.

Now take some time to think about your key relationships and what they could look like in the future. I have suggested some potential people to start with, but only you know who is most important to your success. The results of the worksheet are important, but the thinking, visioning process itself is most important. This is a tool to build self-awareness and motivation, so do not get stuck in the boxes. Use this worksheet to imagine a *picture* of what you want to accomplish: what does the equivalent of "the next Thanksgiving" look like for you?

Person/Group	From ...	To ...	Vision/Values/ Benefits: Strong-Flexible-Fair
My manager			
My team members (complete for each team member)			
My peers (my leadership team)			
Key customers (again, this may vary by customer)			
Functional and support teams			

To reflect upon and imagine a new and different vision for yourself is a powerful way to move toward making that vision a reality. Please be sure to have engaged with this exercise and have these notes in hand before reading on. In the next chapter we are going to build on that "why" by exploring *how* to achieve your vision and build more resilient business relationships.

It's time to get out the hammers and nails, as it looks like we have some work to do.

PART TWO
REFORMING AND MAKING NEW CHOICES

Chapter Four

WHAT'S THE PROBLEM?

N ow that you have crafted that vision of *why* you specifically want
to change your key business relationships so that they become
more resilient, let's look at *how* you might begin to realize that
vision. To begin with, pick one of the most important but potentially
at-risk relationships that you detailed in the worksheet from the last
chapter. We will use this as your own real-life relationship project and
a vehicle for you to begin applying the concepts of strong, flexible, and
fair that we're about to look at more closely in this and the following
three chapters.

But before we begin digging in, what do you think is one of the
biggest differences between leaders who understand the importance
of relationships and those who do not? Among all of the leaders I
interviewed for this book, I found one consistent difference, which
was that they created a *practical strategy*. As Christine Landon
pointed out:

"Leaders need to assess where people are and whether it's appropriate to do relationship building … with certain people you have an immediate connection—but even if you don't— you have to create it over time and *intentionally* build that into all your interactions with that person."

If you are one of those people who've always believed that success is more about how smart you are rather than having effective relationship skills—think again. Research conducted by the Carnegie Institute shows that we would rather work with people we *like* than people who have a higher IQ. So it's your social and emotional intelligence, your "EQ," that really counts. Consistently using an intentional relationship strategy at work will accelerate the development of your EQ.

Intentional relationship strategies have these three components:

1. Clarity about the "end game" or the desired outcome: this is a definition of the goal or desired future state. Please look back at the worksheet from the last chapter—the "To" column.
2. Clarity about how the game is played: a clear understanding of what is driving the behavior of the people in the relationship (the current relationship dynamic), which is the subject of this chapter.
3. A plan to succeed: the actions and principles that will move the relationship from breakdown to breakthrough. You will learn more about this in later chapters.

The good news is, you are already well on your way to creating your own relationship strategy because of the work you did in the previous chapters.

Having the awareness and making the choice to design relationships *strategically* can be a real challenge for most people. Many leaders and managers feel that it's sufficient to be focused solely on business or technical goals. They're the ones hoping, if they give any thought to this issue at all, that all this relationship "stuff" will work itself out over time.

I must admit that for a good many years I achieved a certain measure of success with that kind of approach myself. My mode of relating used to be rather like the salesperson who uses the same approach with everyone they meet, regardless of who they are or at what stage in the buying process they are. I was like the pathetic salesmen in the movie *Glengarry Glen Ross* who acted on the advice to "Always be closing!" I had to have an instant rapport or else I quickly moved on to someone else. At the start of my career I did in fact "hit it off" with some people but not with others, which meant that I was leaving my relationships up to luck.

The leaders whom we most admire are typically those people who create goals for their relationships. They have a set of skills and principles that they use to determine where their relationships stand today, and they then decide what *actions* they can take to move those relationships closer to their goals. These leaders make sure that every action they take will do double duty—moving the business goals forward *and* enhancing their relationships. What you need now is a way to think about *why* your relationships may not be as strong, flexible, or fair as they need to be. You need a model that is quick, clear, and actionable so you can move forward with each interaction. And the model you are about to be introduced to in this and the following three chapters has precisely those qualities.

If Hope Is Not a Strategy, Which Strategy Works?

Just as good salespeople know that not everyone is at the same stage in the buying process—some are ready to sign as "qualified leads" while others remain "prospects"—good leaders vary their approach to relationships based on what the dynamic requires.

For all business relationships, there are three key strategies you can use to build resilience. By understanding how to use each of these strategies you can make your relationship stronger, more flexible, and fairer, and shift the dynamic from breakdown and into breakthrough.

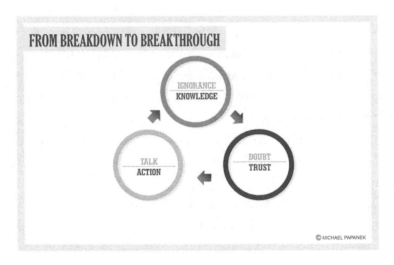

These strategies will be used to describe the relevant dynamics in your relationships in this and the following three chapters. By understanding where a relationship is positioned on the model, you can then determine how best to proceed. In short, these strategies are a tool to focus on the underlying problem in the relationship and develop a practical solution to move the relationship forward.

The three strategies are framed as key "shifts," or changes, in the relationship dynamic:

Ignorance to Knowledge: Is the breakdown in this relationship caused by a lack of knowledge about who each of you really is at a deeper level? Is this causing false assumptions about the other to be made? How can you learn more about who each of you really is at a more personal level, so you are interacting as real people and not just roles? The better we connect with each other as people, the easier it will be to take risks and survive setbacks.

Doubt to Trust: Is the problem concerned with uncertainty or even fear about each other? How can you build trust and become more confident that your interests overlap? Remember, trust is always tested during change and stress in organizations.

Talk to Action: Is the problem one of too many meetings and emails and not enough action? At some point we must test the relationship and either see that it is moving in the right direction, or it's not. Do our actions tell the same story as our communications? Relationships require effective communication, but actions always speak louder than words. What are your actions telling others?

Dave Rolefson, Director of Global Alliances and Strategic Partnerships at Google, has used all three of these strategies and his story provides an illustration of how to move through each of them.

After working within a previous role at Google, Dave applied for and got a new position in sales finance. During the interview process, Dave met the two people who would report to him as well as his direct supervisor. What Dave didn't know at the time was that those two team members had also applied for the position he had been selected for! Before Dave's first week on the job, these two direct reports threatened to quit because they were offended that someone who had not moved up through the ranks had come in over their heads.

One of them told Dave that she had a job offer from another team and challenged Dave to tell her why she shouldn't take it. The other person wanted to know why Dave's job hadn't gone to him. During some preliminary discussions, it appeared that both of them were concerned that Dave would claim credit for their work. Their concerns about potential failure were not without merit, since their group was under intense pressure to complete a plan for senior managers, who were known to be very hard to please.

Here is how Dave's situation maps out using the three strategies:

Strategy	Current State Assessment
Ignorance to Knowledge	Dave and the team members had not worked together before. Each was making assumptions without any real understanding of the other's actual goals or needs. The team members were considering actions and making claims based on these false assumptions.
Doubt to Trust	The team feared Dave and his lack of experience in their area. Dave feared the team members would either leave or not give their all if they were forced to stay on.
Talk to Action	Neither Dave nor the team members were confident they could still reach their goals. Progress on key deliverables was stalled.

The bottom line was that the team was already in the process of breaking down. This could have been a very difficult time for any new leader. What would you do in this situation? How would you go about avoiding sliding into breakdown?

Here is what Dave did, in his own words, to turn breakdown into breakthrough:

Strategy	Actions
Ignorance to Knowledge	"I approached each team member directly and asked them about their careers and what they wanted personally to achieve. I let each person know that they could still get those things done working with me. We discussed my strengths and what I believed I could bring to the table to help reassure them that success was feasible."

Doubt to Trust	"I went all out to form a strong relationship with the top executive of our group. I leveraged that trust to help highlight the work of others on my team. I was also good at translating the feedback I got from that executive and used it to inform the direction I gave the rest of the team. As they presented their work it became clear to everyone that their efforts were highly regarded and each person felt that they were getting credit where it was due. Everyone began appreciating that I was helping them raise their value."
Talk to Action	"I focused on getting the work done to give our relationship a chance to form. I asked everyone to make the same commitment that I was making and I ensured we made changes along the way as situations cropped up that we didn't like. I told them: I will assume the best about you if you will do the same for me. I pointed out that we had to work as a team for this to work."

As you can see, Dave took the time to assess the dynamic of these relationships that were headed into breakdown mode. He then used each strategy to determine the best course of action and was able to transform what could have been a disaster for all concerned. They were able to form a cohesive team and became life-long allies who helped each other later in their careers.

As Dave described the outcome: "Now, years later, I still have very tight relationships with both of those team members who had threatened to leave. I even ended up promoting one of them to director, just before I left the group. They saw that I was able to provide my own kind of value, which was not about detracting from their worth and efforts. In fact, I demonstrated just the opposite, which was to highlight what great work they were doing."

Now let's compare Dave's actions to the three components of an effective strategy:

1. Clarity about the end game or desired outcome: Dave chose to define "winning" as having an effective team where everyone succeeds, where he is able to add value without taking anything

away from others. His "personal why" (see Chapter Three) was to build his brand as a team leader who helps others succeed, gives credit to others where it is due, assumes the best in everyone, and addresses issues head-on.

2. Clarity on how the game is played: Dave knew that in his organization's culture (as in most others) excellence and results are greatly valued, and the question of who gets credit is naturally very important to those who put in the effort. It's great to be in a meritocracy, but not if some leaders grab credit and increase their importance by diminishing others. The currency of this game was results, acknowledgement, and future opportunities. If the employees believed Dave had their best interests at heart, he would "win," and if they did not, his department would crater and fail.

3. A plan to succeed: Dave's plan involved two key actions. First, Dave chose to always give his team very accurate and clear feedback, based on what the top leader of the group wanted, so that they could react and improve over time. At the same time, he gathered and acted on their feedback to him. This built trust that Dave could provide his team with what they needed to be successful. His other key action was to keep his promise to make sure the right people got the credit for these team improvements. And he avoided counter-ultimatums, threats, backstabbing, and excuses for not getting things done, at all costs.

In order to be able to build resilient relationship under stress and change, you will need to become very good at assessing the dynamic of a relationship, forming a strategy, and then executing to achieve results.

The Benefits of a Relationship Strategy: Victory from Defeat

Now imagine what would have happened if Dave had not had a practical framework with which to understand his relationships when starting in his new role. What ended up as a clear win for everyone could have quickly turned into an intense conflict. That would have taken much more energy, with Dave focused on reducing the risk of losing his team, rather than having the freedom to address his business goals in a positive way. Just like Christine at Workday, Dave employed a relationship strategy and was able to keep his talented team intact, enhance everyone's reputation, and secure promotions and growth for everyone. You would not expect to succeed in any enterprise without a business strategy, so how can you expect to succeed as a leader without a relationship strategy?

Dave was able to realize the benefits of focusing on both business outcomes and resilient relationships:

- No surprises: Dave was able to prevent the loss of key team members.
- No blind spots: the biggest challenge to successfully moving up the ladder in organizations (according to many of the top executives I work with) is lack of self-awareness as to how we are perceived by others. Dave made sure to get the feedback he needed.
- Gaining influence: by being open to the needs of others without defensiveness, Dave built the credibility and respect he needed to influence them.
- Shifting the heat curve: trusting relationships have a stronger "container" and can hold more heat safely.
- Quick recovery from setbacks: relationships that are strong, flexible, and fair bounce back from challenges because people value the relationship too much to let it fail.

- An attractive leadership brand: attracting others who also value resilient relationships, creating a culture of resilience across the team.

Now, I hope you have been thinking about one key relationship of your own as you read about Dave's experience. Taking a clear hard look at your relationships can be tough, but this awareness is key to the next steps. Over the next few chapters we'll focus deeply on each of the three core strategies mentioned earlier, using more real-life case studies, so you can become a master of resilient relationships that not only survive, but also get stronger under stress and change.

Now that we have taken the ten-thousand-foot view of the three strategies for building resilient relationships, we are going to move down to ground level to discover how you can think about and use each of them to build your own resilient relationships. The next chapter will be especially relevant if you suspect that your project relationship is based on ignorance versus knowledge.

Chapter Five

FROM IGNORANCE TO KNOWLEDGE

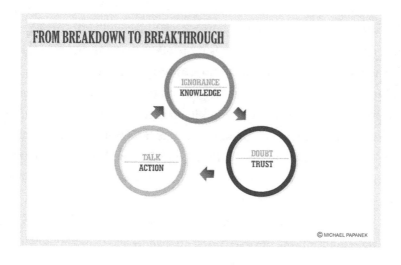

"First you build relationships, then you build a business."

—Warren Buffett

We have all experienced joining a new business team or interdepartmental group where, in many cases, there is barely time for cursory introductions before it's down to business. The problem with this scenario is that all you ever learn about your teammates is based on superficial takeaways—maybe the occasional chat over lunch (while looking at your phone) or direct observation (which may not be as observant as you think). All of this leaves you vulnerable to making assumptions about others that may or may not be true.

That's only part of the problem. Understanding and empathy are hard to achieve under normal circumstances; they're even harder to find when everyone is feeling stressed and burdened by deadlines or the shadow of their next performance review. As you may have learned from Malcolm Gladwell in his book *Blink: The Power of Thinking Without Thinking*, we tend to form very rapid conclusions about other people. Within the first few seconds of meeting them we will have "sussed them out" or made an assessment that is more often than not based on biases. We just don't realize how much those assumptions and expectations are influencing what we choose to see and hear. That is why this strategy involves not just shifting away from ignorance but replacing that lack of understanding with a deeper, more accurate, and holistic understanding of the connection between you. Please understand that ignorance is not meant as a pejorative term here, but simply means *ignoring or being unaware of* relevant information.

Now, before we share the case study that illustrates the benefits of making stronger, more flexible, and fairer *connections* with an individual, let's review how ignorance was playing a role in some of the stories you read earlier in this book:

- **Julie and the Zombie Accounts (Introduction):** Because I had always viewed Julie only from my point of view, all the evidence I gathered about how unreasonable she was to work with was filtered through a distorted lens. Everything that *she* did one way or another negatively impacted what *I* wanted. I was so focused on this context of animosity that I barely noticed, let alone responded to, Julie's attempts to connect with me as a person. We only moved out of ignorance and into greater knowledge about each other—and so began to enjoy some mutual gains—when a new context forced me to see her through fresh eyes.

- **Mr. No and the Sign-Off Sheet (Chapter One):** Mr. No had formed some very strong opinions about the people of EDS even before he'd met us. Not surprisingly, I started out being viewed not as a real person but as a stereotype—in other words, another stupid kid from EDS. On my side, I had been prepped by my colleagues to view this man as little more than another worthless bureaucrat from GM. Had we continued to willfully ignore each other as people and only seen each other as designated cartoon characters, we would never have found a way to create a bridge between our mutual goals.

- **Bill a.k.a. Master of the Universe (Chapter Three):** Remember how Bill had no compunction in mistreating many of his firm's personnel, in part because he saw them merely as support staff in a one-man show? Only when Bill was reminded that people at the office needed to be treated with dignity and respect, just like the people in his personal life, did things begin to change.

- **Dave and the Threatened Team Mutiny (Chapter Four):** Dave and his direct reports didn't know each other at all but still harbored assumptions borne out of ignorance. Although they were erroneous, those assumptions were not unreasonable based on what they'd each experienced with similar leadership transitions in the past. That's the insidious nature of assumptions—human beings have this built-in bias to look for evidence that proves them right rather than wrong. It is to their credit that the team members had a high enough EQ to hold those assumptions in check long enough for Dave to have a chance to prove them wrong.

In each of these examples at least one person held erroneous beliefs because they failed to seek out any new information that might help change those beliefs. It is easy to remain stuck in ignorance (it takes so much less effort, right?). But if what we are looking to do is shift our relationship's heat curve up and to the right—thereby ensuring that the relationship is resilient under stress—then we are likely to need a lot more data than we currently have.

Now to the case study example for this chapter that illustrates one method for connecting with *people* rather than simply focusing on their roles in an organization. From time to time I'll remind you where strong, flexible, and fair fit in, as each of these is essential to shifting a potential breakdown in communication to breakthrough results.

I Found My Heart in San Francisco

San Francisco is a beautiful city that relies heavily on tourism. Those of us who live close by mostly appreciate how the money that visitors spend keeps the local economy buoyant. Some of the biggest spenders are the many trade associations and organizations that hold their conventions and conferences there. As you can imagine, competition for those big business conventions is fierce. The city also needs to make itself attractive enough that the business stays in San Francisco and doesn't go elsewhere. Hence, an efficient and welcoming hotel industry is critical. However, at one point it seemed that hotel staff and management in San Francisco were hell-bent on shooting themselves in the foot.

Sad to say, the hotel industry in this part of the United States has a long history of difficult labor-management relationships, although things are much better now. During the mid-1990s, when this story occurs, strikes by hotel workers had become not just more disruptive but also more frequent. The result was that the organizers behind some of the biggest national conventions began to look at venues outside of San Francisco. And you couldn't blame them. After all, no conference organizer wants to face high-paying, irate attendees who complain about people banging pots and pans outside their hotel rooms at all hours of the day and night as part of ongoing picket line activities.

My firm was hired by the leaders of both the unions and hotel management to help assist with some preliminary negotiation strategies, prior to both sides reviewing and signing their new two-year contracts. Even at this early stage, the heat was on. The US economy was in a downturn, spending on business travel was way down from previous years, and fears about yet another strike led many to believe that some hotels would have to close down altogether, with the attendant loss of jobs and livelihoods. As if that wasn't enough to contend with, San Francisco was already more expensive than many competing cites at a time when conference organizers' budgets had to stretch further than ever. *And* this was an election year for the union officials, who needed to show their members that they weren't backing down in the face of what they perceived as management hostility and intransigence.

If any situation seemed tailor-made for a full-on breakdown, it was this. Let's just say that we were under no illusions, given the history between both sides, that either might choose to bail on us or revert to more confrontational means of getting what they wanted.

As we began to gather some preliminary data from our interviews with managers and workers who would be attending the negotiations, a pattern began to emerge. Each side appeared to hold some very definite beliefs about the other, which informed their behavior. For example, the workers tended to be recent immigrants or first-generation Americans; most had limited English and had not been educated in the US. When we asked them what their relationships were like with hotel management, they implied that collaboration was impossible, "because they have no respect for us." On the other hand, the managers tended to be born and raised in the US, were college-educated, and few spoke any language other than English. With considerable disdain, they would confide how they "didn't know what kind of people" they'd be asked to supervise.

Their current relationship type was "coercive" because it had only one of the three characteristics of a resilient relationship. The union-management relationship was strong—because the work they did was important and created value for all parties—but it was not fair or flexible.

So far, so bad.

Next up we needed to address some of the key contentious issues that would be front and center in negotiating the next round of contracts. These included pay, work scheduling and hours, grievance procedures, and so on. We formed working groups made up of equal numbers of people from union and management, from a cross-section of the hotels involved. Each working group was tasked with reaching consensus on a proposal for dealing with their particular issue. We needed these recommendations to be included in the formal contract negotiations so that the later negotiations would run smoothly and lead to agreement.

I was the facilitator for one of the working groups that had been asked to thrash out issues concerning housekeeping. On the union side were representatives of the people who repaired and maintained the rooms (known as "housemen"), as well as the maids who cleaned and stocked the rooms. The management participants were mostly first-line housekeeping supervisors who worked for a number of different hotels in San Francisco.

When I entered the room for the first meeting, I thought someone had turned up the air conditioning full-blast, the atmosphere was so chilly. Managers sat on one side of the room, workers on the other (you've seen that happen, haven't you?). Neither group looked at the other, let alone attempted to talk. Each gave the impression that they were about to reenact the Civil War. These were people who had worked with each other for years, without really knowing much about each others' lives. Each individual was seen not as a person but only as their role: houseman or supervisor. Everyone seemed to have formed the impression that the "other side" could not be trusted to bring about a mutually beneficial result.

Knowing that everyone in that room had come together to get into the meat of the issues concerning housekeeping, what would you have done to kick things off? Let's briefly recap what we faced:

- Two groups who were certain their interests were mutually exclusive, even though most of them had never had a direct connection with one another, and had formed their opinions based on what others had told them. Given their level of ignorance about each other, they were sitting in that room assuming the worst.

- Management thought that the unions wanted to avoid work, while the unions thought the management wanted to exploit them. Historically, they had learned (and had their beliefs reinforced over time) that the only way of "negotiating" anything was to blame the other side for any problems.

- Both groups obviously felt that the truth was not a safe thing to share. Based on experience from prior negotiations, each side had seen how information had been used against them. Yet, as Will Schutz wrote in *The Human Element*: "You cannot go anywhere new until you tell the truth about where you are."

We were on the vicious cycle to breakdown. We needed to shift from ignorance to knowledge before we could attempt to work creatively together.

But how?

Listening to the Whole Person

To kick things off, we made a list of the issues that the working group wanted to include. That way everyone could see what our joint scope and purpose were, as well as know that their individual interests would be on the agenda. Remember what we said about strong relationships and how they have a shared purpose and values? Because it was so straightforward, the list-making was the easy part. But at least we were beginning to embed some small degree of "strong" between these groups.

To everyone's surprise, I then suggested that we spend some time connecting and getting to know each other on a personal level before we went ahead with the main business of the day. And here's where I cheated a little bit.

My goal going in was to persuade each person in the room to share information about who they were: their families, how and where they grew up, and what brought them to work in the job they now held. I had hoped that each speaker would reveal something personal and meaningful about themselves and not just do the usual business equivalent of name, rank, and years on the job. That way each listener could get a better sense of him or her as a whole person.

Before you start to tune out, thinking that this kind of *kumbaya* is fit only for scout troops and church gatherings, let me point toward recent studies of doctors treating diabetes, which found that doctors who communicated with patients less by telling and more by listening and being empathetic achieved better health outcomes. In one study reported by The Mayer Institute[13] in 2011, Dr. Gary Rodin, an oncologist at the University Health Network in Toronto, noted that the outcome of diabetes treatment can be particularly affected by a doctor's empathy. "Diabetes control involves a lot of attention to insulin dosage, exercise,

---

13   Frank Appleyard, "Empathetic Doctors Have Better Outcomes in the Treatment of Diabetes," Postmedia News, March 9, 2011, http://www.themayerinstitute.ca/empathetic-doctors-have-better-outcomes-in-the-treatment-of-diabetes.

diet and lifestyle. That involves collaboration between the patient and the physician, and the interaction has a big difference in outcome," he said. "Empathy and communication are tied together, and those allow a more collaborative relationship with the patient."

Here I do not mean the "nice meeting" kind of listening, where everyone politely waits his or her turn but no one says anything really important. This is listening with the intent to learn, teach, and build deeper understanding.

So the idea for these introductions was that we would take turns between union and management team members. And here's where the "cheating" occurred. I had prepped two people in advance (one from management, one from the unions), not only so that the room wouldn't stay silent for too long once I'd made the invitation to share, but to nudge them into being more honest and vulnerable than might otherwise be the case, in order to model a deeper exchange for the listeners.

As you read these two stories, one from a houseman and one from a housekeeping supervisor, imagine yourself holding the stereotypical views attributed to the "other side." Notice how you feel and what changes.

The Houseman ("Nguyen"):

Nguyen and his family had come to the United States from their home in Vietnam to escape the oppression of the Communist government. In his own country, Nguyen had been a skilled and experienced aircraft engineer who had worked for the airlines maintaining commercial jets. When he came to the US, our airline industry was just deregulating and cutting back on jobs. Unable to get hired within his profession, Nguyen took his current low-paying, lower-skilled job as a houseman in order to support his wife and children. He had held this position at the hotel for the past two years.

The Supervisor ("Frank"):

Frank's college degree was in Hotel Management, but when he had started work for this chain it was as a busboy because there were no management openings at the time. He held that job for a year before moving into management. During the three years that Frank had been in his current supervisory position, his employer had relocated him to different states three times. His work required him to spend ten hours a day or more on the job, mostly with no overtime. It was partly for these reasons, Frank said, that his wife had recently divorced him, taking their three young children with her. Nevertheless, Frank loved his work and dreamed of one day becoming the general manager of a hotel in New York City.

As we began to hear more and more similar stories, of professional and personal challenge, sacrifice, and passion, something in that room shifted. We stopped acting from pre-designated roles and became real people again. It was as if the spirits or souls that we had left on the other side of the door had been reclaimed; it was remarkable to watch the people in front of me transform away from the frosty reception of just an hour or two earlier. How did I know this change was real? Because of everyone's body language. People who previously couldn't look each other in the eyes were now smiling and nodding at each other as they recognized experiences that were similarly meaningful to them. In short, everyone was beginning to become more flexible.

Remember what we learned about being flexible: it marks the shift away from "I" to "we," away from rigid positioning and expressions like "my way or the highway," and toward an understanding of the needs of others. Rear Admiral Grace Hopper once said, "The most dangerous phrase in the language is "'we've always done it this way.'" As the members within the room gained greater appreciation and understanding of each other as people, they became incrementally more flexible and less inclined to fixate only on their own needs and what they expected from this meeting. They became willing to be influenced and to compromise; they were now more open to sharing ownership of the outcomes and to change how the game was typically played.

How was this achieved? Well, let's unpack the stories of Nguyen and Frank. Through honest and open sharing—remarkable in itself given that each had entered this room expecting the enemy within—we could see the similarities in their experiences, whereas before we only imagined the differences. By virtue of being vulnerable in telling their stories, each earned the respect of their peers. Through Nguyen's revelation of his professional past, supervisors began to realize that "low-skilled" referred to the position, not the person. And that often professionals like Nguyen, who was unable to secure employment that leveraged his talents, had accepted employment that did not fully represent what they were able to achieve.

With respect to Frank's story, the union members were able to see that having a role in management wasn't always the "cushy job" they imagined it to be. As the union and management members heard more and more of these stories, questions were raised by both sides about why the organization was not more open to tapping into the ideas and perspectives of the highly intelligent, valuable talent pool populating many of these so-called "low-skilled" jobs. And, in some cases, we railed at any industry that would expect their managers to make so many personal sacrifices for their jobs with such a small chance of long-term reward.

Familiarity Breeds Respect

Psychology journals are full of studies documenting how much harder it is to mistreat someone, or to be mistreated, if the people involved know each other as individuals. Stanley Milgram's famous experiments conducted at Yale beginning in 1961 revealed the extent to which an average person, who otherwise thinks of him or herself as fair and decent, is capable of harming a fellow student when asked to do so by someone in authority—especially when they cannot actually see the other student experiencing the pain.

In a variation of Milgram's experiment, Stanford professor Albert Bandura further highlighted the impact of preconceptions and bias on relationships. In his 1975 study, Bandura arranged for an assistant to refer to a group of students as "animals" and, in another condition, to call those same students "nice." After overhearing such remarks, the student participants in this study who had heard the other group referred to as "animals" were significantly more likely to deliver what they believed were increased levels of electric shocks.[14]

And in case you think (or at least hope) that human beings have come a long way in the past forty-odd years, consider that in some cases of cyber-bullying, many resulting in the victims' suicides, the perpetrators admitted they committed mean acts because there was no direct connection between them and their victims. As one *Psychology Today* article pointed out: "A cyberbully does not necessarily see the reaction of the victim, making it easier to engage in mean behaviors."[15] An article on cyberbullying in *The Atlantic*[16] tells how two young boys who had been threatening a girl online reacted when they learned she was a real person who was scared and upset by their threats:

---

14   Melissa Dittmann, "What makes good people do bad things?," *Monitor on Psychology*, October 2004, 68. http://www.apa.org/monitor/oct04/goodbad.aspx.

15   Michelle Kilpatrick Demaray, "Why Do Some Kids Cyberbully Others?," The Wide Wide World of Psychology (blog), *Psychology Today*, April 26, 2013, http://www.psychologytoday.com/blog/the-wide-wide-world-psychology/201304/why-do-some-kids-cyberbully-others.

16   Emily Bazelon, "How To Stop The Bullies," *The Atlantic*, March 2013. http://www.theatlantic.com/magazine/archive/2013/03/how-to-stop-bullies/309217.

"At first the boys railed against Ash [a person who had asked them to stop bullying the girl] on Twitter, and one played down his involvement, denying that he had ever threatened to rape the girl. But after a while, two of the boys began sending remorseful messages. 'For two solid days, every time we logged on, we had another apology from them,' Ash said. 'You hear a lot of lies and fake apologies, and these guys seemed quite sincere.' Katherine thought the boys hadn't understood what impact their tweets would have on the girl receiving them—they hadn't thought of her as a real person. 'They were actually shocked,' she said … [One boy] said that at first, he thought the girl's account was fake; then he assumed she wasn't upset, because she didn't block the messages he and the other boys were sending. Then Ash stepped in. 'When I found out she was hurt by it I had felt horrible,' he wrote to me in an email. 'I honestly don't want to put anyone down. I just like to laugh and it was horrible to know just how hurt she was.'"

As you begin riding the heat curve, all of these insights about connection are especially important. In times of stress, de-humanization of the "other" often becomes the default dynamic—that is, unless you make a conscious decision to change that. Better still, ensuring that you know each other in a deeper, more meaningful way than typically occurs in business contexts, particular combative ones such the one I'm describing here, helps to overcome the problem in the first place. Just be aware that the kind of knowledge we're talking about in this chapter must be deeper than some of the team-building approaches that are often used. A quick "How was your weekend?" exercise or "Tell us something we do not already know about you" might be fun and valuable when resilient relationships already exist and the heat curve is already strong, but under the stress and change of today's business environments, something more is required if knowledge is going to make the relationship stronger, more flexible, and fairer.

Speaking of which, what of "fair"? Would you think it more likely that the groups began to see each other as having greater potential for fairness now that they had connected in this way? Now they had shifted from the ignorance of their original positions (unions versus management; college versus high school diploma—if that; "us" versus "them") to some semblance of knowledge about their whole lives, aspirations, and passions, can you see how fairness just fell into place, almost magically?

Let's see what this looked like as our group shifted away from the introductions and began settling down to the business part of our meeting:

Ignorance	Knowledge
Recognizing no value	Appreciation of the value created ("strong")
Assuming that the other side "has it easy"	Understanding that many shared (or similar) challenges put us in "the same boat" ("strong")
Assigning the worst motivations for others' actions (money, greed, stupidity)	Acknowledging the range of motivations that drive complex business situations ("flexible")
Seeing power as a zero-sum game	Being willing to be influenced and to share power in the service of jointly desired outcomes ("flexible")
Lacking trust	Trusting that benefits, outcomes, and other value will be appropriately distributed ("fair")
Viewing everyone else as having created the problems	Recognizing that people are doing the best they can and it is the context that is creating the problems ("fair")

As this chart outlines, and the story I shared with you illustrates, shifting from ignorance to knowledge does not have to be a long, drawn-out process.

What we each need to be wary of, however, is allowing technology to usurp the experience we need to have, face-to-face, one-on-one, warm body to warm body, for true connection to take place. Certainly, computers allow us to make connections these days with anyone just about anywhere, but this kind of connection is superficial at best. Phone, Skype, WebEx, even video or advanced "TelePresence" (a highly realistic video conferencing system from Cisco) all separate us somewhat from the human element that is fundamentally important to this part of the breakdown to breakthrough process. Consider a study by Kevin Rockmann of George Mason University and Gregory Northcraft, a professor of executive leadership at the University of Illinois. After measuring two teams, one that used video and all the latest "lean communication" tools, and another who met face-to-face, they found the face-to-face team had higher trust and more productivity. According to Northcraft, "Technology has made us much more efficient but much less effective. Something is being gained, but something is being lost. The something gained is time, and the something lost is the quality of relationships. And quality of relationships matters."[17]

Time to Make Some Deposits

Once the members of our working group had shifted from ignorance to knowledge, the rest of our work moved along efficiently and effectively. We successfully proposed a revision to the formal grievance process, which was replaced with one-on-one feedback and communication.

---

17 Belinda Luscombe, "Why E-Mail May be Hurting Off-Line Relationships," *Time*, June 22, 2010. http://content.time.com/time/health/article/0,8599,1998396,00.html.

This proposal was included in the final round of contracts and, thanks to the efforts of the other working groups, we were able to avert a costly strike.

As Stephen Covey famously said, "Relationships are like bank accounts, you have to make deposits before you can make withdrawals." True, you might manage to call in some proverbial loans in your relationships without spending the time to form a true connection. But as we know from trying to balance our budgets in difficult times, when times get tough those favors dry up faster than a puddle in a Texas summer. *Now* is the time to make a clear assessment of your level of connection with your key relationships and make sure your accounts are fully funded. That way you will have the means to make whatever withdrawals you need to when times are lean.

Over to You ... the Introduction Exercise

Here's where you get to put what you have just learned into practice. Keeping in mind the relationship you have selected for your relationship project, please give the following exercise a try right now in order to start to shift toward deeper knowledge of that person.

If you had to introduce this person to a room full of people and wanted to make an inspiring, exciting, and authentic introduction that would be remembered by the audience and appreciated by the person being introduced, could you do it based on what you know about them at the moment? Would you be stuck with only the usual (and boring) items anyone would know: "Sara has been a project manager in the support team for three years. I understand she also has a great collection of mugs on her desk ..."?

If you realize you could not introduce them in any meaningful way, try this: in your next meeting with this person, make sure to take a few minutes off the business agenda to ask them more about who they are and what makes them tick. What do they love most about their job? What had they aspired to be when they were growing up? Where did they grow up? If they could design their perfect day, what would that look like?

Try to go deeper than the basics: ask about something they have done that they are especially proud of or excited about. If you can meet them in their space (office or cube), you can ask about something you see in their work area to get things started, like I did with Mr. No. If you want to go really deep, ask: "What would you be willing to share so I can get to know you better as a person, not just in your role as X?"

Obviously the degree of intimacy is something that will unfold, but look to ask them more interesting questions in order to gain more interesting answers. Sure, they might be a bit surprised initially, especially if the two of you have never said more than "Hello" outside of business meetings, but remember that most people are happy to talk about themselves. Be sure to show genuine curiosity so they don't think you're just being nosy or checking off some arbitrary relationship box from a list of leadership attributes. Find out about their real life story: where did they grow up, how did they come to be in their current job, what do they enjoy or care about outside of work?

You are likely to find this simple exercise to be a gratifying experience for both of you. Just remember that you are not doing this just so they will ask about you; resist the temptation to turn the topic to yourself. Then go ahead and write a short introduction about this other person for the time when you might be called upon to do so—in a way that shows that you have made a significant deposit in the relationship bank, one that will pay off time and again.

Remember that by making a fuller, complete, and human connection, you are building a container for heat and change. That container will be needed during the next strategy for building a resilient relationship: shifting from doubt to trust, which is the subject of the next chapter.

Chapter Six

FROM DOUBT TO TRUST

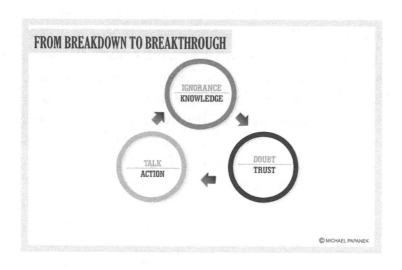

"The chief lesson I have learned in a long life is that the only way to make a man trustworthy is to trust him; and the surest way to make him untrustworthy is to distrust him and show your distrust."
—**Henry L. Stimson**, former US Secretary of State, Secretary of War

When was the last time you worked with someone whose abilities or motivation you doubted? Perhaps you found yourself wasting considerable time and energy double-checking their work, verifying that they were on track, or just generally stressing out about whether key objectives would be achieved. If you were lucky, you might have had the option of *not* working with or for this person in the future. Most likely, you had no choice.

Many surveys point to an epidemic in business that can spread like a disease, infecting you, the members of your team, even your whole company. What we are talking about here is a lack of trust. For example, the Forum Corporation's Leadership Pulse Survey found in 2013 that 34 percent of employees trust managers less today than in the past and only 8 percent of employees said they trust their leaders "to a very great extent."[18] At only 8 percent, there is clearly room for improvement!

But what do we mean when we use the term "trust"? In a *Harvard Business Review* article entitled "The Decision to Trust"[19], Fordham University professor Robert Hurley defined this as the "confident reliance on someone else when you are in a position of vulnerability." Such confidence is predicated on a sense of safety and predictability that the other person or group will act in your best interests, even when that might require sacrifice on their part. Rather than a gut decision, or one

---

18   Abby Smith, "Is the Leadership Trust Gap Hurting Employee Engagement," Forum (blog), November 11, 2013, http://www.forum.com/blog/the-leadership-trust-gap.

19   Robert Hurley, "The Decision to Trust," *Harvard Business Review*, September 2006, https://hbr.org/2006/09/the-decision-to-trust.

that just forms over time, Hurley found that we decide whether or not to trust someone based on the following factors:

The Decision to Trust Model

Low	**Risk Tolerance**	High	Trustor Factors
Low	**Adjustment**	High	
Low	**Power**	High	

Low	**Situational Security**	High	Situational Factors
Poor	**Communication**	Good	
Not Demonstrated	**Benevolence**	Demonstrated	
Conflicting	**Alignment of Interests**	Aligned	
Not Apparent	**Similarities**	Apparent	
Low	**Integrity/Predictability**	High	
Low	**Capability**	High	

Distrusting Choice   **Trusting Choice**

Decision to Trust Model © Dr. Robert Hurley

When building resilient relationships that are strong, flexible, and fair, it's vital to shift the doubt you have, or others may have about you, to a greater sense of trust. Great leaders know this. One of the most dramatic examples of inspiring the trust that helps to create resilience occurred during Sir Ernest Shackleton's voyage to the Antarctic starting in 1914. His boat, the *Endurance,* was crushed by ice, capsized, and sank. Shackleton's crew did not reach solid ground for 497 days, yet everyone survived. All because their captain never doubted they would make it through together, even with all the odds against them. Shackleton's relationships with his crew were so resilient—meaning strong, flexible, and fair (for example, Shackleton would never eat until his crew had eaten)—that the team almost willed themselves to survive.

Similarly, in her books *Unfear: Facing Change in An Era of Uncertainty* and *Lemonade: The Leader's Guide to Resilience at Work*, Karlin Sloan researched the impact of a leader's belief systems on their ability to deal with stress and challenge, and found that the most resilient leaders believe that "things will work out." They have confidence in their ability to act and be effective, and are likely to succeed even when faced with setbacks. In that respect, they have what Slone calls "unfear." This confidence—that the worst-case scenario is rarely the most likely one—helps them to lessen, even eradicate, doubt. This attitude engenders a sympathetic response in others, creating a positive dynamic where people who feel trusted act in more trustworthy ways. As Ben Franklin said when exhorting his fellow revolutionaries to continue to stand united against all odds, "we must all hang together, or we shall certainly all hang separately."

Yet operating separately due to a lack of trust was certainly prevalent in the stories we've discussed throughout this book:

- **Julie and the Zombie Accounts (Introduction)**: Remember the doubts I harbored about Julie's role at my old firm, including her lack of experience? My lack of involvement in hiring her, and her direct and personal connection to one of the senior partners, made me distrust her motivations, intentions, and capabilities. Only when I changed my attitude toward Julie from "enemy" to "client" did we start to build a more trusting relationship.
- **Mr. No and the Sign-Off Sheet (Chapter One)**: Mr. No had much to doubt about me: I was fresh off the bus and barely out of programming school, yet was now in charge of critical

systems. My lack of track record, and EDS's arrogant attitudes generally, must have seemed like a very dangerous combination to him. Similarly, I did not trust Mr. No's intentions.

- **The San Francisco Hotels Scenario (Chapter Five)**: In this case, the unions and management did not believe they could trust each other, and believed that each side was acting against the other's interests. Only when someone had the courage to be transparent did they shift toward trust.

In each of these stories, the lack of trust, even fear, seemed justified initially, but turned out to be a barrier that people had mostly created for themselves. By understanding why people choose to trust, leaders can take actions that will create trust and pull everyone together under stress so they do not turn on each other.

So that's the challenge under the spotlight now. As you think of the key relationship you are using as your personal project for this book, let's look at how you can shift from doubt to trust and in doing so transform a breakdown relationship to one that achieves continuous breakthroughs—even under conditions of stress and change.

But before introducing a case study to illustrate this phase, let me insert a practical note.

I am not saying that everyone can or should be trusted. We've likely all been burned in our business dealings over the years, and berated ourselves for foolishly trusting another person or persons. It's a tough world out there and we cannot be naïve. Having said that, I've also learned that usually all that is needed to build a trusting relationship is to change my own orientation. Rather than judging the other person and hoping that *they* will change, you can usually shift the dynamic by changing your *own* behavior. In the end, the times we should have trusted and did not sting even more than those times when we did and got screwed as a result.

Mad Men

John, a senior director at a large insurance company, had a sizeable problem. An analysis of the organization's IT spending had shown that 90 percent of the budget was being spent on "maintenance"—simply keeping all the old systems running—and only ten percent on updating capabilities and implementing new systems. The IT group within this insurance company was seen as outdated, disorganized, and out of control. If they did not make improvements quickly, the CIO decided, they were going to outsource all of IT and disband the department, impacting over one thousand jobs.

That's when external contract consultant Robert was brought in. He was hired to assist with some important technical aspects of the change. Robert had successfully orchestrated this kind of project many times before, and his technical knowledge was going to be crucial in helping the firm leapfrog to state-of-the-art systems. Similarly, John had been with the firm for many years, and was trusted by others to handle the legacy systems fairly.

In short, both John and Robert had the right skills and experience for the project and were committed to doing whatever was needed. The problem was that they just couldn't get along. Their relationship with each other was getting in the way and threatening to set back, if not crater entirely, the transformation project. Both had shown real leadership by stepping up to a high-visibility, highly complex, and high-risk project. But instead of banding together to get the job done, they were working apart and even against each other. Their heat curve clearly sloped down and to the left (any heat and they would break down). Neither felt the relationship was strong, flexible, or close to fair. I'm sure you have seen this scenario yourself before: two good people who were entirely capable of doing great work, if only they could get along. These situations tend to end one of two ways: either they get their act together, and often become one of the strongest partnerships around, or someone leaves—voluntarily or otherwise.

In this case, neither man trusted the other, and not without cause. Robert had gone ahead and held some important meetings without John attending, and John was concerned that high-level decisions were being made without his involvement. John, for his part, doubted Robert's motivations, thinking that this arrogant, pushy, disrespectful, and power-hungry consultant (in John's view) was out to make him look bad and weaken his influence. He was perhaps partly right, as Robert believed that John's team was a big part of the problem. Robert had even shared this point of view with the CIO, word of which had—of course—made its way to John. What emerged was a vicious cycle of blame and excuses.

I could go on at length at the sense of indignity that each of these two very capable professionals felt when their abilities and motivations were being so publicly doubted and disparaged by the other. But you get the picture. You may well have seen this kind of "us versus them" behavior play out in your own organization; you may even have had the unfortunate experience of being one of those involved. Let's just say that with respect to John and Robert's relationship, things were starting to get ugly. As much as they hoped to, neither was going to get the other one fired.

The real tragedy was that they were both very productive and did add value, but could have and needed to produce so much more. Robert had worked with the CIO before, and was trusted by him to complete the project and get the new systems up and running. John was accountable for long-term management of the systems after Robert had moved on. Since they needed to work together to achieve the goals of the change, the relationship had to succeed. Yet the strength—in terms of net value produced—of their relationship was limited by a lack of fairness and flexibility. Their inability to trust each other was wasting time and energy while adding drama to an already complex change effort. That's when I was brought in to see how doubt could become trust.

I began by observing them together to see for myself what the issue was. After sitting in a meeting between the two of them, I debriefed with John, who had a very different take on his conversation with Robert than I had. Certainly Robert had a much more confrontational communications style than John and the other internal managers, and had not flexed much to match the culture. But in my opinion he hadn't said or done anything that justified John's strong negative feelings. To the contrary, I saw Robert trying to defend himself against a series of attacks that John had launched into, right at the beginning of that meeting. From my more objective point of view, John's lack of flexibility had made it almost impossible for Robert to remain open and trust that his suggestions would be heard and executed upon.

Changing Results by Changing Attitudes

At this point let me introduce you to a simple formula I developed for just such scenarios, which looks like this:

$$T = \frac{f(I \times C)}{Risk}$$

Let's define each part of that equation.

Trust (T) is: the decision that it is safe to give power over my interests to another party. This determination is "f," a function of three key factors:

Intention (I): Evidence (rather than assumptions or beliefs) of what is driving the other person's behavior: Do they appear to have your interests in mind? Do they seem to be following a set of ethical values? Are they transparent in communicating the rationale for their actions? As "I" increases trust increases.

Consistency (C): Evidence (rather than assumptions or beliefs) showing actions matching their words: Do they regularly meet their commitments? Do they keep these commitments under changing circumstances, especially ones involving stress and difficulty? Are they honest and open to feedback, even about mistakes or failures? As "C" increases trust increases. These two, I and C, are a function because if either one is zero, the numerator is zero and there will be no trust.

Risk: Evidence (rather than assumptions or beliefs) concerning the critical nature of a successful outcome and the impact of failure: What is at stake if we succeed or fail? How stable is the environment? How well can you predict what will happen? Risk is the context in which trust happens, the bigger the risk, the more I and C you will need to still build trust.

At this point I worked with John, applying the trust formula to his relationship with Robert. Again, I stressed the value of relying on evidence rather than just John's assumptions or his beliefs about the other man. Here is what we discovered:

Intention: Robert seemed to be executing exactly what the senior executive team wanted him to do. After all, he was under considerable pressure to achieve results quickly. If Robert's methods appeared unreasonable, perhaps this was because he was being asked to bring about change at breakneck speed. In which case, the "fault" (such as it was) lay more with the internal leadership rather than with the external consultant. John also acknowledged that in terms of his value, Robert's work product was always very high-quality; he took extra time, even under pressure, to create the best value possible for his client.

Consistency: Once we embraced the likelihood that Robert was simply trying to keep his job by meeting management expectations rather than deliberately setting out to undermine John, we reviewed his actions. We found nothing out of line with Robert's stated goal of successful and rapid transformation, a goal that John also shared. Robert had always met his commitments on time, often without the support and sometimes with active resistance from his "colleagues" in the client organization. Robert could be abrasive, but he kept his word.

Risk: By setting aside his concerns with respect to Robert's abilities and motivations, John could see how much was at risk for Robert, as well as himself. Robert lived on the East Coast and left his family Monday through Thursday to work with this client, yet was always reachable on the weekends and on West Coast time. Robert had agreed to an outcome-based contract for this work, meaning that he would not be paid for his time, but only on the completion of specific deliverables. If Robert was not able to make the transformation successful by the deadlines in his agreement, it was likely that he would barely break even, given the time and expenses he had incurred. Rather than feeling like a victim of this external contractor, John began to see Robert with more compassion, as someone with common struggles and goals.

After we had taken some time to discuss these various alternate explanations for Robert's behavior, John began to see how he had been unfair to Robert. Once we had achieved that small breakthrough in John's thinking, we decided to embrace a strategy for building trust between them.

Originally, John had wanted me to help him create a plan to force Robert to change. That is typically our default—the sense that we are right and the other party is wrong, and if only they could see the error of their ways then we could set the world right. Mark Twain knew this when he said "Nothing so needs reforming as other people's habits." But we all know that in our heart of hearts that is not very fair to expect, and is not how we would want to be treated.

By taking this first, small step in objectively, as far as humanly possible, and open-mindedly examining the underlying reasons for the lack of trust between them, John was able to test whether changes in his own behavior could help shift the relationship from mutual doubt to shared trust. I agreed with John at that point that if he was doing all he could and things still did not improve, we could reserve the right to "escalate to management." To John's credit, he agreed to give it a try.

Our reluctance to see our relationships through fresh eyes reflects what Chris Argyris at the Sloan School of Management at MIT called a "reflexive loop." This occurs when each person in a relationship is taking actions based on an existing set of assumptions and conclusions. They dismiss anything that does not fit these assumptions and only focus on data that supports their existing beliefs. This same phenomenon was true in the San Francisco unions example from the last chapter. We know from recent breakthroughs in neuroscience that our brains physically create these reflexive loops, which then become stronger over time. This is known as "neural binding" and actually forces out alternative views. Senior Lecturer Peter Senge and his colleagues at MIT's Sloan School of Management saw this process as a "Ladder of Inference" which we "climb up" as we interpret information.[20] The more we climb the ladder, the faster we can do it next time. Like a muscle getting stronger from use, the loop becomes the path of least resistance in the brain. The more this loop is activated, the stronger the connections get, and the harder it is to build new pathways of thought. In the case of John and Robert, we had in fact *two* reflexive loops,

---

20   Peter Senge et al., *The Fifth Discipline Fieldbook: Strategies and Tools for Building a Learning Organization* (New York: Currency/Doubleday, 1994).

each amplifying the other, creating a powerful breakdown dynamic. This was a leadership opportunity—someone had to try to shift the dynamic from doubt to trust.

John began testing out his building-trust strategy in his next conversation with Robert. When he reported back to me afterwards, he was very excited: "I think something has shifted," he told me. "When I started by acknowledging the goals and challenges we both shared, Robert became much more open to my ideas. I was even able to discuss how I felt about his going behind my back. He said he understood how I felt and promised not to do that again. For my part, I committed to agreeing to living up to my side of the bargain by doing all I could to avoid becoming a bottleneck. Most important of all, we agreed that from now on, no matter how uncomfortable it might be, we would each go directly to the other with any feedback and concerns."

What this set of exercises allowed John to do was to develop a new relationship with Robert that was strong, flexible, and fair. And, remarkably, as John started to treat Robert as someone he trusted, Robert responded in kind—just as the quote from Henry Stimson at the top of this chapter articulated.

Doubt	Trust
Questioning the others' goals and intentions	Acknowledging shared goals and intentions ("Strong")
Being unwilling to take complete ownership and accountability for outcomes, blaming others, or avoiding responsibility	Each person is 100% accountable for shared goals, with no excuses, and shared ownership ("Strong")
Lack of confidence in capabilities, skills, and resources, especially if the person is under stress	Knowledge that each person has value to add and will do whatever is needed to keep their commitments ("Flexible")
Relying on statements and communications that may be inaccurate or biased	Each party will tell the truth and the whole truth, even when it is difficult ("Fair")

Fear that self-interest will drive behavior rather than common goals	Confidence that each party's needs are taken into account when making decisions ("Fair")
Actions do not seem to reflect ethical values	Actions are based on ethical standards and are always consistent with shared values, even when it is inconvenient or costly ("Fair")

John and Robert now began working together as trusted partners and became a force of nature. They not only were a more productive team, but also served as a model for others to follow. We didn't realize it at the time, but the culture not just for that project, but within the company as a whole, had been one where external consultants were regarded as just short of the Devil incarnate, a necessary evil. But after the success of this collaboration, subsequent projects revealed that internal and external teams could work together as trusted partners

Indeed, this experience with Robert also had an impact on John's other relationships at work and even at home. He is now able to notice when he is acting from his doubt-based reflexive loop, and instead use a new attitude: one of trust, empathy, and compassion for the other person.

The Power of Trust

If you have ever felt under threat or experienced long periods of high stress like John and Robert, you know that feelings of doubt, uncertainty, and fear can become habits even when they are no longer justified by reality. This doubt is like the rickety chair in the metaphor from our introduction: you have to sit in it, but you cannot trust that it will hold your weight without collapsing. This is not a pleasant state to be in for any length of time. The evidence of how high-doubt and low-trust work environments cost organizations is dramatic. Fordham University's Professor Robert Hurley also found that environments engendering low trust were described as "stressful, threatening, divisive, unproductive and tense," while high-trust workplaces were "fun, supportive, motivating, productive, and comfortable."[21]

This data is in stark contrast to the Silicon Valley vision of a small trusting team changing the world. Low-trust environments impact that industry as well. According to one Silicon Valley executive I have worked with for years:

> "The issue of trust is very relevant in the high-tech industry because some engineers based their circle of trust simply on narcissism. That creates a barrier for many people … it's really sad that some of these engineers have such individual egos that eventually the only person who is in their circle of trust [is] themselves."

The power of trust is such that it shifts the heat curve strongly up and to the right, allowing a business relationship to function under much more heat. Over time, trust becomes the container for relationships that maintain strength, flexibility, and fairness.

Over to You … the Fresh Eyes Exercise

Here's where you get to further practice your leadership and accelerate your mastery of resilient relationships. Next time you're meeting with the person you are reviewing for your relationship project, or anyone who presses your buttons, ask someone else to be there to observe you and later give you feedback. Maybe they are someone who is in the meeting anyway, or who could naturally attend but doesn't always do so—like your manager, a peer, or a team member. The observer can be almost anyone, as long as you will respect his or her input later.

---

21 Robert Hurley, "The Decision to Trust," *Harvard Business Review*, September 2006, https://hbr.org/2006/09/the-decision-to-trust.

In the same way that I was able to provide a fresh point of view for John, receiving unbiased feedback from a third party whom you trust and who is not invested in the relationship can be extremely valuable. As they watch and listen, have them assess the different factors in the trust equation:

- Based on your behavior, what would the observer assume your intentions are? Do you seem to be watching out for both your own and the other person's interests?
- How open, flexible, and fair do you seem to be? How transparent and honest are you?
- To what extent might you be protecting yourself and attacking the other?
- What risks do you seem to be willing to take or not take, and why?
- How consistent are your words and your actions?
- Finally, what suggestions would the observer have for action you could take to increase trust and reduce doubt?

Your job when getting the feedback is to *stay down your Ladder of Inference* and be open, flexible, and ready to act. The success of this exercise depends on the same Awareness—Choice—Change process that Scott used (see Chapter Two). Remember, the best way to change outcomes is to change your own behavior, and the most effective way to change your behavior is to change your thinking!

Up to this point, most of what we have covered has been about communication and awareness—and a lot of talk. But resilience is created through action. In the next chapter, I'll help you see how the actions—or inaction—you are taking may be contributing to breakdown mode. And how you can get back on the path to breakthrough by making one simple but important shift.

Chapter Seven

TALK TO ACTION

"A little less conversation, a little more action please
All this aggravation ain't satisfaction-ing me!"
—**Elvis Presley**, 1968, from the film *Live a Little, Love a Little*

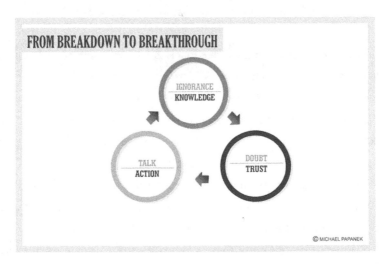

88

D oes this scenario sound familiar? Your change effort is stalled and so your CEO calls another all-hands meeting. The subject is her Vision For (fill in catchy name of new initiative). The CEO and her communications team have been working non-stop on the slide deck. They have high-quality graphics, charts, and compelling stories. The working theory is that the reason the change is not happening is that people are not buying into the vision, so they need to hear it again. The strategy is to over-communicate and tell people to tune into "WIIFM" (What's In It For Me). The CEO has been practicing the speech and is looking forward to answering any questions that might remain so you can finally all get on board. I have witnessed this in companies from Yahoo! to US Steel over the years, and I am sure you have too.

You may already know where I am going with this: the problem is that after the meeting you all go back to your desks and nothing changes. When the reality of what is happening is so far removed from the nicely formatted vision slides, no amount of all-hands meetings, talking points, and cascading messaging will make much difference. Breakdown occurs when leaders focus so much on refining and repeating their communications that they miss opportunities to create real evidence—through action—of what they stand for and where the organization is going. Worse than that, often things are happening in the organization that provide evidence *contrary* to the stated values and vision. It's as if these leaders feel that since making real change is so hard, they would rather work on something that's easier to control, like the slides and the catch phrase. These leaders are essentially rebranding without changing their product, because rebranding is simpler and feels like progress.

The same thing happens when individuals, teams, or departments are so focused on talking that no one gets to grips with what really needs to occur in order to build resilient business relationships: taking concrete action to create breakthrough results. Up to this point we have seen how certain changes in your mindset and mode of communication can create deeper connections and increase trust. This has been a core focus of this book because experience has taught me that too often all combative parties need to do is to shift their heat curve up and to the right so they can talk about the hard stuff more productively. They often discover that their issues can be resolved with more authentic conversations and a change of mind.

However, this is not always the case. Sometimes we've done all we can to make a connection and increase trust, yet the relationship still fails to produce results. While the first two strategies are important, they're sometimes still not enough. You will not have a complete set of tools to work with until you have embraced this third, and maybe most important, strategy: shifting away from talk and toward action. The right action at the right time can sometimes be the fastest way to increase resilience and avoid breakdown. Even if you end up confirming that the relationship will not work as you had hoped it would, you are still better off, since in the real world you cannot expect to have a resilient relationship with every person and you have limited time to waste on a relationship that will never be what you hoped it would.

Without testing the relationship, you will be like an investor who never knows when to sell, holding on to a falling stock and unwilling to face facts. Think of this as *action learning* for the business relationship. As Kurt Lewin said: "If you want to understand a system, try and change it." You must ultimately choose which relationships you want to continue to invest in and which relationships you cannot expect to ever really "pay off."

It may seem obvious that we must act and not just talk, but some organizations have such a tendency to talk rather than act that they have a phrase employees use to describe it: "The Company Nod"—as in "The Clorox Nod" or "The Kaiser Nod." The "GM Nod" has been cited as one source of the problems with GM cars and the delays in recalls. The "nod" concept refers to the following scenario: you suggest an idea at a meeting, everyone agrees "that's great," but then no one carries out the action items. You then call another meeting, everyone again says they will get right on it, and the cycle repeats—as time slips away. Either some senior executive finally sets some hard deadlines, or the idea and its potential benefits just fades away, like fog on a sunny hillside, a victim of "death by delay."

Liz Guthridge, a leadership consultant, suggests[22] that an emphasis on communication over action might have played a role in GM's years-long delay in acting on safety information:

"It's telling that GM sponsors a program called 'Speak Up for Safety,' not 'Act Safely.' Even speaking up for safety is hard to do for some GM employees. They fear they could lose their jobs by raising safety concerns, as noted in an internal GM report, which Congress has received.

By contrast, when Paul O'Neill became CEO of Alcoa back in 1987, he proclaimed 'SAFETY: Zero Injuries.' That was hardly a communication campaign. Instead, it was a habit loop that changed employees' behavior and transformed Alcoa into a streamlined aluminum company. As Charles Duhig wrote in the best-seller *The Power of Habit*, every time someone was injured, the unit president had to report the injury to the CEO within 24 hours with a plan for making sure the injury would never happen again . . . Yes, you need to communicate, but you also need to take actions."

This tendency to see change as communication and not action may in part be due to years of leaders having been told that when people

---

22   Liz Guthridge, "Why 'SAFETY: Zero Injuries' succeeds and 'Speak Up for Safety' fails." ConnectConsultingGroup.com (blog), June 24, 2014, http://connectconsultinggroup.com/why-safety-zero-injuries-succeeds-and-speak-up-for-safety-fails.

resist change the leader just needs to "gain more buy-in" through more dialogue about "the burning platform" or "the case for change." Ultimately, we need to step off the cliff and see what happens, or else we are paralyzed by forever seeking alignment. As Doug Conant, former CEO of Campbell Soup, has said: "You can't talk your way out of something you behaved your way into. You have to behave your way out of it." The Ladder of Inference tells us that *evidence creates belief*; your leadership brand is ultimately based on what you do, not what you say. Let's look once again at some of the case studies from previous chapters to see how the Talk to Action strategy impacted the dynamic of each of these relationships:

Dave and Google (Chapter Four): Dave needed to connect and build trust through communicating with his team, but he avoided a major breakdown—losing his top team members—when he kept his promises by giving credit to his team and not just to himself.

John and Robert (Chapter Six): Robert said that he wanted to work with John, but when push came to shove, his initial actions showed that it was more important to him to move forward and hold on to control than to be collaborative. Only when Robert actually stopped scheduling meetings that John could not attend did he provide real evidence that collaboration was a priority.

Julie and Michael (Introduction): I'd always said that I was collaborative, but then I never supported any of Julie's ideas. Only when I actually took the list of "zombie" accounts and contacted every one of them, demonstrating in good faith that I was following through—even with an idea I did not completely support—did I show Julie I had changed and really meant to keep our agreement to be partners.

The old adage that "actions speak louder than words" is the foundation of this strategy. Here is how you make the shift:

Talk	Action
Reaching agreements	Keeping agreements
Gathering feedback	Acting on feedback
Communicating	Decision-making
Focusing on input	Focusing on results
Documenting the vision and goals	Assigning resources to the vision and goals
Crafting values and mission statements	Applying values and mission when making decisions
Planning	Doing
Trying to change the people	Changing the situation
Explanations, excuses, blaming	Fixing what is wrong
New awareness	New choices
Stakeholder input	Stakeholder influence

Now consider the following real-life example of how the Talk to Action strategy was used to shift relationships and transform a change effort from being in danger of breaking down to producing breakthrough results.

"Thanks for Nothing"

The internal Information Technology (IT) department of a very large heath care provider in San Francisco needed to replace the old system they used for managing customer service requests, which they called "trouble tickets." The old system lacked current capabilities, and was slow and expensive to operate. A new system would allow customer service technicians to provide more accurate estimates of when issues would be resolved, and enable them to measure and report the results more quickly. Most importantly, the new system promised to give everyone the information they needed to solve the *root causes* of the trouble tickets, rather than spending all their time chasing down the status, re-entering due dates, and not having much time for actually solving the issues.

The upgrade of the request system was part of a number of simultaneous changes that were intended to make the whole IT department more solutions-oriented and increase their value to internal clients. Peter, a highly experienced and respected manager, had been put in charge of implementation of the new system.

Peter and his team spent months gathering specifications and building alignment with the many stakeholder groups, which included customers (the ones with the service requests), the tech support team (who processed the requests), and the different management teams whose systems were involved. Achieving the goals of the project would require intense cross-functional collaboration, so Peter spent a lot of time up-front, building the many relationships he would need. There were a few features—like data analytics—that would have to wait until after the initial implementation, but everyone had been warned about this.

Sounds like they were doing everything right, doesn't it?

But here's what happened at the first meeting after the implementation: the executives focused on a new feature of the reports, the green, yellow, and red codes showing the "status" of the service request. Rather than problem-solving, the new information was used to punish, shame, or otherwise attack the tech support people. No one seemed interested in the underlying root causes. The reports were, in practice, a new tool for executives to pressure the tech support team. The meetings devolved into "blame-storming" sessions (discussed in Chapter One) where people had to defend their numbers. This was received by the tech team as evidence of their worst fears about the new system.

The talk had all sounded great, but the action provided evidence to the contrary. The executive team said they were simply looking for some "quick wins" and protested, in even more meetings, that they didn't want to "blame anyone." But they were in fact being unfair to the tech support teams. For example, some small departments might have had very few requests. If a tech support manager had three requests in their department and only one was late, the report showed that 33 percent of their requests were in the red, making the numbers look really bad compared to teams who might have hundreds of requests. In another example, technical routing issues meant that vendors sometimes wouldn't see a request for three days after it was submitted, so every request in their area showed as three days "late" before they even got it!

Everyone involved in the project now had the worst of all worlds: they were all working even harder, but had not improved the business outcomes and were blaming each other instead of working as a team. All these problems just increased demand for meetings to do even more planning and explaining, since in this organization's culture the first step in most crises was to "call a meeting!" All this was happening while a number of other projects were impacting the same people, so the stress level—and heat—was already way up.

At first the resistance of the various stakeholders who used the system, both those who placed requests as well as those who processed them, perplexed Peter and his project team. But they soon realized that holding more meetings "to get better buy-in" would be the definition of insanity—doing the same thing over and expecting a different result.

The reality was that the relationships Peter's team had built with his key stakeholders were not strong, flexible, or fair. They were not strong in terms of creating value, since almost no new improvements were being identified or resolved. There was very little in the way of flexibility embedded into the new system, as Peter's team did not have the resources to change the reports or the processes to match the users' needs. Plus, there was a sense throughout the IT department that the negative feedback they were getting was not at all fair, since everyone felt that they were being judged and blamed rather than supported. The situation had to change quickly or the whole project was at risk of failure. Indeed, some users were already going around the new system to get their issues resolved, which would only make the reporting even less accurate.

When Peter first contacted me, it was so I could help design and facilitate a meeting where Peter and his manager would (again) tell the support teams to "stop feeling so persecuted" and ask them to "take more accountability." Management was sincere and could empathize with the support teams, but needed them to "get on board." To me, this was a plan for making things worse, not better. I asked Peter if he thought any of the tech team's concerns were valid, or were they just trying to avoid blame? He admitted that many of their concerns were justified and that he could understand how they felt. Now was the time to start showing empathy through action. As the *Ketchum Leadership Communication Monitor* pointed out in 2014, "In crisis situations, it is critical to offer practical, accountable solutions that match words and deeds, while operationalizing empathy—rather than simply showing empathy for its own sake."[23]

So, we cancelled the meeting he had in mind, and instead decided that it was time to employ a strategy that shifted the focus away from talk and toward taking concrete action. Peter created a list of the key issues, and directed all of his limited resources to making improvements to the actual work processes, systems, and reports. This involved canceling the dreaded status meetings and focusing efforts on actually resolving barriers to customer service requests. Peter did not share this new plan with the tech support team or the customers, as he was concerned that this would just sound like more promises and talk. So, while the storm raged around them, Peter and his team stayed focused, rolled up their sleeves, and got to work.

Peter changed the metrics so that everyone had the same measures and targets. He completed the data analytics work they'd postponed so

23   Ketchum Inc., *Ketchum Leadership Communication Monitor*, May 2014, page 18, http://www.ketchum.com/leadership-communication-monitor-2014.

they could run analysis of trends and identify systemic issues faster. Peter even found the resources to modify the reports themselves, based on the input from the users and management, so they were less open to misinterpretation.

By focusing on action, Peter was able to shift from breakdown to breakthrough. As a leadership team, his group stopped trying to end resistance by telling people how to feel, and created a new reality that actually caused people to feel differently. Peter's shift toward action caused those who had been complaining to shift toward action as well. When the tech support team saw real change based on their input, they had little choice but to start to believe that Peter had been sincere in his desire not to punish. They started to adopt the system and even attended the trainings, since now they viewed the new system as a path rather than a barrier to better performance. Having stopped talking a good game and playing one instead, Peter became a model for others to follow in a culture that had long accepted lip service instead of action. Refusing to go to meetings with senior leaders because he was too busy doing the work was seen as a revolutionary act! In the past, "too many meetings" was always an acceptable reason for delay. Peter broke that dynamic and, through action, let everyone know there was another way.

Here is our summary of how Peter used the strategy of Talk to Action to save his project:

Talk	Action
Telling people we empathize	Creating evidence by allocating resources ("Strong")
Asking users to adjust to the system, even with its faults	Changing the system to address the user's needs, one step at a time ("Strong")
Listing to feedback in meetings	Acting on feedback ("Flexible")
Holding training classes for people who are not following the process	Changing the process to serve the people involved ("Flexible")

Telling other people to stop making excuses and take ownership	Holding yourself accountable by addressing what is in your control ("Fair")
Asking for what your team needs	Giving stakeholders what they need first ("Fair")

Based on the case above, you might be wondering: if action is so important, why would you bother spending any time building connection and trust? Why not skip all of that and jump straight to letting your good deeds speak? For an understanding of the risks of that approach, consider our next case, about a new manager who finds herself in a very tough spot and, due to a superficial focus on action, fails to take advantage of an important opportunity.

The First—and Last—Ninety Days

In this case, a recent MBA graduate named Sara had been selected for a management development program at Cisco. The program provided new high-potential managers with an accelerated path to advancement and included a number of rotation assignments, each three to six months long, which would take place over a two-year period. Sara's first rotation was to lead a sales department that had a poor reputation. Indeed, they had failed to meet their revenue goals and the previous manager had been fired. Sara would only be there for three months and wanted to have as much impact as she could during that short time. She also wanted to ensure her first assignment laid the foundation for her planned rapid assent up the hierarchy. The culture of Cisco has a well-known bias toward action and results, so Sara was feeling the pressure from day one. She saw this as a test and she wanted to get an A.

Let's pause for a moment and ask, based on what you have learned so far, what would you do in her position? Would you focus on building connection, creating trust, or taking action?

Sara believed she would not be able to shift from ignorance to knowledge or from doubt to trust across this thousand-person organization in just three months. She felt the next, permanent leader would need to do those things, but she would not have time—and anyway she wanted her brand as a leader to be about results! So Sara decided that in her short time there she would focus only on actions she could take, no matter how small, to move the short-term metrics of the team. She would have only one question: "How can I help you change the numbers?" and then she would do whatever she could to get whatever that was for the team.

Certainly Sara was successful in addressing some of the easier issues, but she never really learned the root causes of the department's failures. In terms of relationships, she was well-*liked* by most of her direct reports, but since she decided she would not have time to form deep connections and to build trust, she never created resilient relationships that could handle any heat. Since people did not feel connected, and doubted they could trust her, she never heard the truth from her team about why they had been in trouble in the first place. She did not understand the Will Schutz principle from his book *The Human Element*: you cannot go anywhere new until you tell the truth about where you are.

Sara missed a key opportunity to create her brand as a leader who could lead effective dialogue and then act. Her "fresh eyes" could have launched a fresh start for the department. Instead she turned over the department in essentially the same state as she found it. Taking action for its own sake, without understanding the situation, is just as foolish as not taking action at all.

Now Over to You: The Silent Communication Exercise

The following simple but powerful exercise will give you an opportunity to test the value of this strategy for yourself.

Think about the same relationship you have been working on using material from the previous chapters—or choose a different one: to what extent does the talking that goes on match the behavior you exhibit?

Start by asking yourself: if someone took into account only your actions, with no explanation, what would they conclude about your goals and values? Be sure to think of this from the perspective of the other person, and remember that your own Ladder of Inference will bias you. You will need to develop this ability of self-observation if you are ever going to improve your overall self-awareness, which is the first step in any change. Make a list of any gaps or breakdowns between what you intend and the current reality. For example, Peter's list of gaps would include "lack of accurate or fair data" or "no analysis of root causes." Now ask, how does that match with what you would want the other person to conclude? This list will point you toward areas you can act on to close the gaps between what you want and what is really happening.

Now make a list of any stakeholder input you have received yet failed to act on, for whatever reason. Is there feedback you might be ignoring or refusing to accept? For Peter, this might include "changing the rules so vendors and internals all see the same dates," or "getting better data so we can understand root causes." This list provides areas you can address that will show you are willing to "give before you get." If you have been waiting for others to do something before you address their issues, remove that constraint. To lead literally means "to go first."

Looking at your lists, select no more than two or three actions that you, or your team, can take on over the short term that will provide *silent evidence* that you are willing to take the next step to see if the relationship can move forward. This does not have to be something grand or showy; it should be something you can do relatively quickly that will make a difference and prove you mean what you say.

Remember, resilient business relationships that can implement change come from a combination of strength, flexibility, and fairness. Instead of asking yourself, "What can I tell them?" when faced with a relationship that is heading for breakdown mode, ask yourself instead, "What can I *do*?" to create more value, be more flexible, and be fairer?

Now take the action to do whatever it takes to get these items completed. Find the resources or say no to something else. Maybe there are some meetings you can cancel? Silently communicating—by creating new facts and experiences—will test if the relationship can become more resilient, or if another approach will be needed. And you will know that you really tried: not just to communicate, but to give the other person what they are asking for.

Now that you have learned each of the three key strategies for shifting from breakdown to breakthrough—From Ignorance to Knowledge; From Doubt to Trust; From Talk to Action—let's bring everything together in one practical, actionable process that you can use over and over to build business relationships that thrive in a VUCA (volatile, uncertain, complex, ambiguous) world. For which, please turn to the next chapter.

Chapter Eight

SHIFTING THE HEAT CURVE

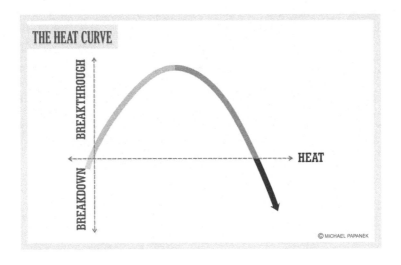

THE HEAT CURVE

BREAKTHROUGH

BREAKDOWN

HEAT

© MICHAEL PAPANEK

We have covered a lot of ground in Section I and the previous chapters of Section II, looking at each element of resilient business relationships and three discrete strategies for shifting your most important relationships from breakdown to breakthrough. Now, to end Section II, you are ready to put all of this to work in the real world and make a difference with a key client, employee, colleague, or manager. How are you equipped for your task?

You have:

- A new mindset, new frameworks, and a clear picture of why you want to change.
- A new self-awareness of how your actions and beliefs impact your business relationships and an understanding of the payoff you can get from changing.
- Already done some action learning, tested these new ideas, and hopefully are seeing some differences in your key relationships.

The purpose of this chapter is not to give you anything new, but to help you use all we have covered so far to produce a plan for moving one of your key business relationships from breakdown to breakthrough *right now*.

How will it work? You will complete a set of simple, targeted worksheets and exercises, creating a plan for change. These are the same worksheets I use as an executive coach and leadership consultant, and to create strategies for my own most important business relationships. These tools, along with the theory you've already absorbed, will help you efficiently develop a practical and informed plan.

This will be an active chapter that will need your participation. During this chapter, you will:

1. Assess a critical relationship you are concerned is in breakdown mode.
2. Identify the most important gaps you need to address to achieve breakthrough.

3. Identify the current relationship type and where you want to focus.
4. Develop an action plan to close those gaps and create a relationship that can thrive when the heat is on.

Let's get started.

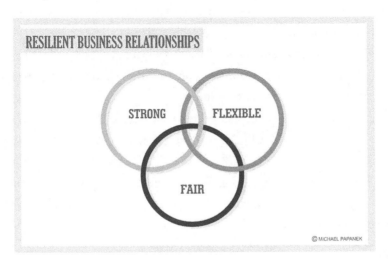

Assessing a Key Relationship for Resilience

First, let's select the relationship you would like to change. This may be the same relationship you have been using so far in the book, and if that's the case, you might want to look back at the other worksheets you have already completed before moving forward. Or you may want to focus on a different relationship at this point.

These worksheets are similar to the one we used in the Master of the Universe example (Chapter Three) and the Dave at Google example (Chapter Four). You will be asked to assess the current state of the three key attributes of a resilient relationship (strong, flexible, fair):

- Current—what is the current state of the relationship?
- Desired—what would you like it to be?
- Gap—what is the gap between current and desired?
- Bottom line—how would you rank the relationship on a scale of 1 (very low on this attribute) to 5 (very high for this attribute)?

Following through with these steps will ensure you form a complete and thoughtful approach to selecting the key gaps you want to address first. Your strategy will be to focus on the areas that will shift the heat curve up, to achieve more breakthroughs, and to the right, to handle more heat without the relationship breaking down.

Gap Analysis: Where Is the Problem?

Strong: What needs does this relationship contribute to? How important or unique is the value created by this relationship? How broad or limited is the value created? How much synergy exists?

Value
What goals or needs does this relationship meet or contribute to?   • Business: e.g. product, leads, expertise, leadership?   • Financial: e.g. revenue, margin, financing, cash flow?   • Emotional: e.g. affiliation, empathy, humor, feedback?
How much synergy does the relationship have?   • Do you each optimize and extend the other person's strengths?   • Do you exacerbate or compensate for each other's weaknesses?
How important is this relationship?   • Unique (hard to replace)?   • Typical (many sources of this value)?
Bottom line: 1--------------2-------------3-------------4---------------5-------------6   Weak   Strong

Flexible: How easy or hard is it to gain the value created? How many different ways are you able to work together? How does the relationship respond to change? Who makes the rules, and how hard is it to change them if needed?

Flexibility
How many ways do you work together to create value in this relationship? • Only one way? • Many ways? • Is there an open and intimate tone?
How well has the relationship responded to change and stress? • Does not change no matter what? • Changes slowly and with much effort? • Able to change rapidly and easily?
How efficient is the relationship? • Low effort, high output—it's just easy? • High effort, low output—everything is a struggle?
Bottom line: 1-------------2-------------3-------------4-------------5-------------6 Rigid   Flexible

Fair: How ethical is the relationship? How open is the relationship? How is the value of the relationship distributed? How are power and decision-making distributed? How fairly are differences or conflicts resolved?

Fairness
Do both parties in the relationship share the same values? • Overlapping values—we want and care about the same things. • Exclusive values—we care about different things, but not in conflict. • Competing values—we do not want the same things, and our goals are incompatible with each other.
How trusting is the relationship? • Safety—we can take a risk (for example, exchange feedback) and know it will be OK. • Predictability—we can predict how the other will act in response to events. • Consistency—we have a track record of keeping our promises to each other. • Intentions—we know we have each other's best interests at heart. • Actions—we have proven through actions that we want to be fair with each other.
How is the value distributed relative to the contribution? • In balance—we each feel our rewards are in line with our effort. • Out of balance—at least one of us feels they are not being fairly treated by the other, in terms of what they are giving and what they are getting for it.

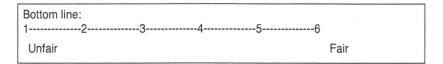

Bottom line:
1-------------2-------------3-------------4-------------5-------------6
 Unfair   Fair

Relationship Type: What Is the Current Dynamic?

Based on your results above, select the current relationship type. Is the relationship:

Strong and flexible but not fair = coercive
Strong and fair but not flexible = tenuous
Fair and flexible but not strong = superficial

Now decide which is the best area to improve first. Should you make the relationship stronger (create more value), more flexible (able to change), or more fair (equitable and balanced)? You might need to improve all three over time, but it is most effective to select one area to start with, so your investment is most likely to pay off.

Your Most Resilient Relationships: Find Your Strengths

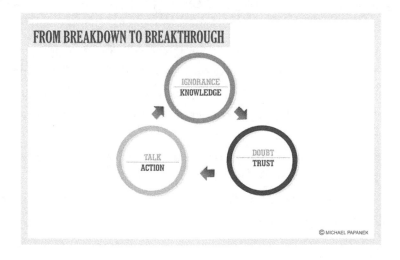

Now that you have a strategy for the relationship, and before you make your action plan, please think about your own most resilient relationships, the ones with a heat curve that can handle the most intense stress. This way we can identify your relationship strengths and leverage those to close the gaps you have identified.

For this exercise, do not confine yourself to your business life only, but consider all areas of your life. No matter how hard it might be sometimes to get along with people at work, everyone has resilient relationships in their life, or has had them at some time. People do not have one relationship type they are stuck in at all times; everyone has and is capable of having resilient relationships, depending on the context. Even someone as difficult as our Master of The Universe Bill, who had mostly coercive relationships at work (strong, but not flexible or fair) had some wonderful long-term relationships in other areas of his life. By noticing what he did to make those relationships work, Bill was able to tap into those same skills and approaches to improve his work relationships, without going against the grain of his natural personality and preferences.

Some of the resilient relationships I thought about from my own life included:

- A fellow member in my rock band—as often happens with musicians, we have had our "creative differences" (like John Lennon and Paul McCartney, only without the talent), but we are still playing together after more than 25 years and sounding better than ever.
- A coaching client—he started as a client who was going through a very tough time and we have since become close friends, proving coaching, feedback, and support to each other as leaders of our own companies.

- A client I first met in the 1990s—she and I collaborated on a leadership program at Silicon Graphics in the early 1990s. Whenever she moved to a new company, she always brought me in as well—at Cisco, Google, and Yahoo. We now have a long record of successful programs and engagements.

- My spouse—my wife and I have been married (as of this writing) more than thirty years. We have been through some very difficult challenges, such as serious illness and large-scale changes, and we are still together.

The following is my list of the tactics I use within an overall strategy of shifting from Ignorance to Knowledge, from Doubt to Trust, and from Talk to Action, which I draw on whenever I'm focused on developing new resilient relationships. You will notice that many of these approaches have also been highlighted in the different cases we have covered so far, such as Julie at my old firm and Mr. No at EDS.

STRATEGY: From Ignorance to Knowledge

STRONG	
	• I am clear about what I really want to get out of this relationship and have worked to understand what the other party wants.
	• I identify my values and purpose and share them with the other party.
	• I ensure we have regular frank and honest discussions about what each of us needs rather than just assuming that I know what those needs are.
	• These discussions are conducted in person at least some of the time.
	• I make arrangements to meet clients and colleagues outside of work in order for us to understand each other beyond the roles we each hold (i.e., we leave our stripes at the door).
	• As such, we move from a superficial connection to a deeper ability to relate.

FLEXIBLE	• I regularly remind myself that I must be willing to be influenced, adapt, and compromise. • I have regular discussions about upcoming challenges with the other party in order to brainstorm how we might head them off together—not necessarily waiting until they happen.
FAIR	• I make sure we meet the critical goals of each party; not just my own. • We do not have "equal" parity, but each person feels they are being fairly treated/compensated, and in proportion to the contribution they make.

STRATEGY: From Doubt to Trust

STRONG	• I earn and give respect, supporting the choices others make without doubting their motives or abilities. • I think in terms of a dynamic relationship system, rather than just two individuals coming together to fulfill a need.
FLEXIBLE	• I am willing to examine underlying beliefs and assumptions (double-loop learning). • I allow myself to be influenced (versus "my way or the highway"). • I share ownership of results (failures as well as successes) without blaming. • I share power and decision-making. • I work collaboratively to build shared solutions that are not imposed but agreed to.
FAIR	• My effort is to win for both sides, not just for myself. • I am willing to give up total power and instead share my goals, intentions, and fears, and to ask for help.

STRATEGY: From Talk to Action

STRONG	• I connect in ways that move beyond discussion and produce strategically focused results that neither party could have accomplished alone. • I make sure to do things together, professionally and personally, that foster intimacy and closeness, and not just talk about collaboration in meetings at work. • I accomplish outcomes of such value that it would be hard for either party to replace this relationship, and both would miss the results.

FLEXIBLE	• I can quickly shift from a current situation that is not working to a new one without it being a long, drawn-out, and high-drama process. I do not see change as a challenge to my power.
FAIR	• I show people through my actions—including the use of resources (like spending sufficient time)—that I care about a fair partnership and keeping my commitments.

Now let's think about those key relationships from your life that have continued even under challenge, stress, and change. They could be with a partner; a best friend from high school, college, or the service; a sibling; a parent; or a teammate. Fill in the worksheet below with the thoughts, feelings, and behaviors you engaged in to get to that resilient place with the other person. How did you build that solid chair you now sit in? This will be the same list you can draw from to change your key relationship today.

Using your own sheet, brainstorm the ways that you have used the three strategies to create your own resilient relationships:

My Strengths: How Do I Shift My Relationships From …
- Ignorance to Knowledge?
- Doubt To Trust?
- Talk to Action?

Your Action Plan for Breakthrough

Finally, using your list of strengths and your assessment, you will identify ways to use each strategy to close the gaps you want to focus on.

Here is an example:

I have a relationship with a coaching contractor who places me on engagements with companies that need executive coaches. I had previously identified the relationship type as "superficial"—meaning it was fair and flexible but not strong:

- Fair—my share of the coaching contract was reasonable.
- Flexible—I could accept or refuse engagements as I pleased and work when I wanted.
- Not strong—I did not get very many engagements, and the contractor did not get much increased business from me.

I enjoy the work I do with this company and they seem to have been very happy with me, but since we haven't done much work together, neither of us has been gaining a lot of ongoing value. The relationship could easily end if the contractor was under special pressure to reduce the number of consultants they use or experienced a downturn in client requests. I decided my best approach to shifting the heat curve would be to focus on improving the strength of the relationship (creating more total value). This would make the relationship more resilient—I could count on them, and they could count on me, if (or rather when) the next economic downturn occurs.

Area to Improve: Strong		
Make Connection	Build Trust	Take Action
• I will meet with the contractors in person. All of our work so far has been virtual. • I will learn about their long-term goals to see how I can contribute.	• I will ask to be on more team (versus solo) assignments, so I can get to know other consultants.	• I will assist the contractor in their marketing and sales efforts and actually bring them a client, rather than only serving clients they had to find.

• I will try to add more value for them (like bringing in new business) *before* asking for something in return (like getting more assignments).	• I will understand and measure their goals as well as my own.	• I will say yes to more engagements with this contractor, even if they are not perfect for my needs.

Now, complete your own chart:

1. Enter the area you want to focus on in "Area to Improve."
2. For each strategy, complete at least one or two things you can do to close the gap.

Area to Improve:		
Make Connection	Build Trust	Take Action

Once you have both a wise strategy and a focused plan for implementation, you can make the most out of each interaction you have with that person. You can even use this as a discussion guide for the next meeting you have with them. The only thing that matters now is to go do it. Remember how lasting change works? You have increased your awareness, you have made new choices, now is the time for actions to create lasting change: for your leadership brand, your short-term results, and your long-term success.

So please go out and do it! I predict you will be very impressed with the results.

This chapter completes Section II. In the next and final section, we will take the resilient relationship principles we have used so far and scale them even higher. You will learn how leaders apply the principles of resilient business relationships to key decisions (like hiring) and then how teams and even organizations can build a culture that supports and encourages resilient business relationships, both internally and externally.

PART THREE

REFREEZING AND LOCKING IN CHANGE

Chapter Nine

LEADING A RESILIENT TEAM CULTURE

W hat does an effective leader do, day in day out, to create an environment of resilient relationships within their own team, across the organization, and with those external to the organization, like clients and vendors? That was what I wanted to know in order to complete this section of the book. To do that, I interviewed four individuals who, to me, exemplified leaders who embrace the concepts of strong, flexible, and fair—even when, in most cases, they have not been directly exposed to the resilient business relationships model. They simply do what they do as an expression of what works and who they already are, a point I hope you will also reach as a consequence of developing more resilient relationships for yourself.

All of our interviewees have also dealt with specific circumstances that contributed to stressful or heated contexts, as outlined below:

- Stig Nybo, entrepreneur and former President of US Retirement Strategy at Transamerica Retirement Solutions. A significant change to his organization also meant a change to his role and sphere of influence. In his new role, Stig had accountability across his organization, while at the same time having a relatively narrow span of control. As reporting structures changed, the new dynamic tested many of his existing relationships. As you will discover, Stig held close to the value of fairness above all else so that he and his team could continue to maintain their breakthrough reputation. You will discover how he went about creating a resilient relationships culture within his team and how he reinforced that with each hire and every team meeting.

- Karen Adamson, Department Manager, Technical Projects at Clorox. In Karen's case, cross-functional teams were needed to accelerate innovation and product development within the company. The new approach required that new relationships be formed, including finding a way to focus on shared goals aimed at supporting enterprise-level goals and strategies, not just functional objectives. You will discover how Karen's team of Research & Development representatives helped to make the new team-based system work by balancing the different tensions that existed among the sales, product, technical, marketing, legal, and finance teams, so that they were resilient enough to achieve competitive breakthroughs in the new, "hotter" environment.

- Karlin Sloan, President and CEO of executive coaching firm Sloan Group International. Successfully growing a small start-up consulting firm into an international coaching practice, Karlin and her team faced daily pressure to create cash flow and meet client needs. As most of us have found at some point in our careers, unfortunately some of Karlin's clients showed that they did not share the same business relationship values—like fairness and mutual gain—that she had. In Karlin's case this meant establishing a more values-based partnership between her firm and the client, so they are not just seen as a vendor filling an order. You will discover how Karlin goes about creating and maintaining resilient relationships, even when it sometimes means firing the client.

- Alan Armstrong, CEO and Founder of Eigenworks. Eigenworks is a global marketing research company that conducts win/loss analysis, mostly for software companies in highly competitive markets. Alan has spent years in the trenches of business-to-business sales and will share with us what he has learned about how both sellers and buyers can launch and maintain resilient relationships (focusing only on price is not one of them!).

But let's kick off this section of the book by focusing on how, as a leader, you can establish a resilient relationships culture throughout *your team*. You'll also learn how to go about ensuring that new team members are the right fit, and how to constantly create the right culture in meetings by modeling resilient relationships at all times.

A Culture of: "I've Got Your Back"

When it comes to leading and developing resilient teams, there was one characteristic I found that the leaders I interviewed all embraced naturally: the "I've Got Your Back" approach.

As Stig pointed out, what characterized his team at Transamerica more than anything else was a feeling of shared responsibility. He developed and nurtured a team culture where creativity, results, and resilience thrived—a combination all too rare in corporate America.

"I used to think it was incumbent on me as the leader to add all of the value, at least in terms of coming up with the better ideas. Because

I thought if I wasn't doing that, I wasn't fulfilling my obligations as a leader," Stig says.

"But what became extremely clear to me is that a big part of being a leader and a viable part of resilient relationships is understanding that a lot of the great ideas will come from somebody other than yourself. For me, the definition of synergy is when you can let the reins go."

In order to communicate that understanding, Stig's entire team was inspired to collectively create a safe environment, first by *valuing* each other and then by backing it up with action. "As a leader I had to have the guts to say to my team, 'You've got to have each other's backs because the alternative won't be tolerated.'"

Stig recognized that there were people who were great at certain things on his team, as well as the fact that there were certain things he personally was *not* great at.

"But the one thing that we always did was support each other. If I ever found somebody not doing that, they knew that was just not negotiable."

The way this manifested in Stig's case was in constantly ensuring that everyone on his team got credit for what they did. "It was such an important philosophy for us—making sure nobody had their thunder stolen—so if any of us missed the mark once or twice, it wasn't the end of the world, because people would say, 'You know what? That was totally unintentional.'"

This echoes the learning of Scott Notebloom, "The Pugilist" introduced in Chapter 3. Consistently giving credit to your team while taking the blame for failures as the leader helps to strengthen the resilience teamwork, particularly under stress, when the "blame game" is most likely to be played.

For many leaders, however, this can be challenging. Not least for those who consider that relationships consist of winners and losers—

even with their own people. For Stig, it has always been a case of setting your ego aside and "not being apprehensive about somebody else outshining you in an area," and recognizing that "you can't be all things to all people."

For example, as a man with ideas that are often so ingenious they won't always initially resonate with the audience, Stig appreciates the fact that he has a team that will protect *him*, as well as him protecting *them*. "One of my favorite sayings is, 'Don't worry, I've got your back,'" he notes.

Playing Fair

Of the three factors within the resilient relationships model, fairness is still the most important personal driver for Stig. Nevertheless, he's realistic enough to recognize this can't be the top priority in every circumstance. For example, he was often required to make presentations for which other team members—or those from other departments—had made significant contributions, yet they weren't the ones recognized publicly. But when the inevitable grumblings go on under the surface, Stig doesn't believe in ignoring them or allowing them to fester. He says, "I've had to personally go back to someone and say, 'You know that's not me; I would never do that purposefully. I get that I *did it*, but it was contextual. Something that was necessary for that environment.'" Since Stig has always had a reputation for being consistently fair, those who interacted with him—especially within his own team at Transamerica—were more than willing to assume the best and understand his predicament. Stig's consistent fairness allows all of his relationships to be flexible, so they can bend and not break under pressure.

Establishing an "I've got your back" culture and reinforcing it with everything you do involves two other important day-to-day activities for leaders: recruiting new hires and running meetings.

Hiring for a High RQ (Relationship Quotient)

One of the biggest mistakes Stig sees with many hiring approaches is to focus too much on whether or not someone has the immediate skillset to do the specific job, rather than placing the greatest emphasis—as he does—on whether or not they're a great cultural fit.

"I think you have to look for people that are consistent with who you are, meaning the values you hold most dear. And it's your responsibility as the leader to make that clear," he says.

Stig adds that while some may choose to "sugar-coat" to entice certain "high flyers" to come on board within an organization, he prefers to do the opposite, telling potential hires, "You know what? Here's how we're unconventional, but we're that way because we like it and that's not going to change." That unconventionality includes it being permissible *not* to get everything right all the time, as well as the mantra that Stig holds dear: having each other's backs.

"What we do and how we do it—those things change with time," adds Stig. "But who we are as people and as a team, including the fact that we always have each others' backs, that stuff doesn't change."

This reflects the real definition of a "value": a true value is something that is so important to us, we would rather lose in the marketplace or go out of business—if we had to—than change.

His interview style reflects a greater focus on the person, rather than the role or their immediate ability to do the job.

"I ask questions like, 'Tell me what your week looks like. When do you get up in the morning? Do you work out? How much of your day involves thinking? What time do you like to go to bed? What do you do in between? How many appointments do you want to have?' It's more a candid conversation than an interview in that respect. I want to get to know who they are and understand how they might fit into our culture. Then I'll dig a little deeper for those traits that will make them successful with us. But the candor works both ways. If someone asks about a product that I know is not fully baked, and we expect their help to create that product, I'll tell them that up front. That sets the tone for them to say, 'You know, I haven't done that before, but here's why I think I can. I know I can do what you're asking.'

"One thing I always emphasize is that it is probably easier to get a job with me than it is to keep it or be successful in it."

The Clorox Way

Karen Adamson of Clorox also creates resilient team cultures by building in "I've got your back" relationships before a new team member is even hired.

"I make hiring a team sport and made sure we had at least three or four other team members involved in the process. I tell them 'Mine is only one data point. I'll have the final decision, but I need to understand what you guys think.'"

Karen knows that involving team members in hiring decisions encourages support instead of competition. "If someone has a hand in who we hire and bring into the practice, they know they have a duty to support that new member, to give them the tools that they need, to coach and mentor them."

This also helps the new member relax when they do join the team, since they know their teammates supported the decision and therefore have a sense of ownership in their success. Karen adds: "Being chosen by your peers has even more weight sometimes than being tapped by a director or a VP, which feels nice for a moment but may not be as lasting. They don't get that strong support from each other once on the team."

Like Stig at Transamerica, Karen looks for key attributes of potential hires to make sure they'll thrive in the kind of mutual environment she leads.

"We don't just focus on the competency around product development, for example, but on teambuilding. We want to know what they're thinking about and so I'll ask them, 'If you were tasked to build a great team, how would you do it? What would you be thinking about?'"

Both are exemplars of the classic "hire for attitude, train for skills" approach. While it may be tempting to hire the "most-qualified" person based on technical knowledge and track record, that's not enough to establish a resilient relationships culture. "The biggest challenge I see at Clorox is that some people who've made it through the ranks got ahead by focusing the spotlight on themselves. They were really good at self-promotion, very good at individual heroics. What we need is for them to completely shift and be successful through an entirely different set of skills, including widening that aperture so they're shining the spotlight on the whole team."

Karen screens for this attribute during the interview process by including questions about teamwork. "We'd talk to people about what their leadership style was or what they appreciate in some of the best leaders they've been working with. Then we would look at the attributes they admire to see whether these are qualities consistent with our culture."

Not *My* Meeting, *Our* Meeting

Sometimes, if things do not go as planned, it can seem easy to expose others' weaknesses, to undermine them or take them down, especially in front of others. It's the Achilles heel that undermines teams from within and it will weaken any resilience you may have. Teams that attack each other will see a crisis as one more chance to score points and avoid accountability, rather than a time to pull together. That is why it's so important to establish an environment that is fair, flexible, and emphasizes the need to stay strong by having each other's backs. And why it's vital to hire those who value such an approach.

Safe environments are where creativity thrives, says Stig. Unfortunately, safe environments are all too rare in corporate America.

For Stig, it goes back to setting your ego to one side as the leader and recognizing you don't have all the answers, all the time. Particularly in meetings.

"If you come into a meeting and the boss has all the answers and it's going to be the boss' direction, I think your outcome is going to be sub-optimal. But if you create a safe environment where people say, 'You know what? Sometimes the boss comes up with nutty ideas, but a lot of them are great ones, and overall we see the vision,' that's a supportive environment, which demonstrates that your people have *your* back, as well as you having *theirs*."

Karen takes an approach similar to Stig's. She reinforces a resilient team culture by making sure she is not the center of every meeting.

"I see a lot of teams are set up in that hub and spoke management model, with the manager at the center, who has individual relationships with each of the people on his or her team. But the people don't necessarily feel very connected with each other. I think my group would certainly never have remained resilient and achieved as many breakthroughs if I had put myself at the center of their universe."

She refuses to give in to the pressure placed on her as the leader by those who expect her to have all the answers or believe it's safer just to do what the boss tells them to do, in order to avoid accountability if things go wrong.

"The telling point in most team meetings is when someone fields a question," she says. "You sometimes have to step back and give others the chance to show how much they know or how much they've contributed. You have to share the spotlight, not hog it completely yourself."

The Art of Delegation

Karen sees meetings as more than just a way to check status or brainstorm ideas. They are also a place where resilient relationships can be *formed*.

Even the agenda of the meeting is an opportunity to build resilient relationships by being strong, flexible, and fair. You can ask team members to take turns facilitating the meeting or designing the agenda and stated outcomes. This not only frees up the leader for other tasks, but also builds ownership and accountability as each team member learns what it takes to make meetings successful, rather than being on the outside able to complain. It is part of leaving space for others to be strong, showing flexibility on how things get done, and fairly allowing others to show influence.

"We usually had one or two people who felt very passionate about what kinds of topics got onto the discourse," Karen says. "Each person had a meeting they were responsible for every two weeks. It was a big shift for people to realize, 'Oh, it's not one where I have to present something. I need to go talk to my peers and find out what's going on, what's hot, what they're interested in hearing about.'"

It's Not About "Nice," It's All About Candid

Stig believes in being candid and transparent with his team in meetings, especially around the concepts of fairness and having each other's backs. Instead of pushing for more personal power, Karen gives more of it away and so gets more ownership and empowerment from her team in return. For Karlin, her team rides higher on the heat curve without breaking down because she uses her meetings as a way to be honest and open about team dynamics.

As she says, "I'm a huge believer in actually discussing team dynamics, because once they're pointed out, they can change. What we have done is to change the dynamic of people being afraid of hurting each other's feelings, because if we all thought we were strong enough, everybody would be pushing to find solutions to our biggest problems."

Exchanging Tough Feedback Builds Resilience

Karlin has found that by coming to the table with the perspective that each team member is valuable, and that the sum of all those relationships is important to your organization, you'll find it worth your while to take the time to talk through things and see a different perspective. In which case, she says, "Things work out. It's so simple and yet most people just don't do it."

For her, it begins by treating people as adults. "You don't hold back criticism because you believe that people can take it. If you respect that people are capable and resourceful and whole, you treat them well and have compassion, then you will say what you think rather than believe they're going to be crushed under the weight of constructive criticism."

To be truly resilient as a team, says Karlin, you need to push each person to become better at what they're doing, not just through cheerleading. "It's about really addressing whatever's wrong and what can be improved and telling it like it is. That takes believing that people have the ego strength to cope with that."

As powerful as it can be to build your own culture of resilient business relationships in your team, if your team is an island in a sea of cut-throat competition and the rest of your organization does not share your approach, what can you do to create resilient relationships with other departments and groups? Our next chapter addresses that question: how can I lead for resilient relationships outside my own team, so I can influence my entire organization to reflect the strength, fairness, and flexibility needed to sustain success?

Chapter Ten

RESILIENT RELATIONSHIPS ACROSS THE ORGANIZATION

I t's one thing to build a resilient team culture among reports over whom you have direct influence: it's quite another to help ensure resilient relationships are a priority among leaders of *other* teams and departments within your organization. Having reached this point in the book, you're presumably sufficiently convinced that organizations that promote resilient business relationships throughout the company have a competitive advantage over those that do not. But we can't assume that your peers, or those *you* report to, think likewise.

So what can you do to scale up your knowledge and understanding about resilient relationships beyond the confines of your own team?

Before I get into that, let me just say that the approach of this chapter is somewhat different from that of Chapter Nine. With interdepartmental relationships, it's less relevant to talk about tactics, such as how to hire for cultural fit, or ways to demonstrate that you've got everyone's backs during team meetings. In this chapter, the focus is on how to influence others' thoughts and behaviors in a way that enhances interdepartmental collaboration. As such, it's more about developing a personal strategy that models this for others.

A Different Approach to "Intent"

It all starts with intent. To be more specific: taking a broader, flexible, and somewhat more forgiving view of the potential intent of the *other* person with whom you are interacting. Remember this came up in earlier chapters when I outlined the stories of me and Mr. No at EDS, with the San Francisco hotel unions, and with the "difficult consultant"? The source of each breakdown was a serious misreading of the intent of the other side.

Let me illustrate this point further with an example shared by Karen of Clorox.

At one time Karen struggled to help one of her co-workers—let's call him Ken— understand that the reason his requests for one-on-one conversations with a key stakeholder in another department—we'll call her Susan—were continually being canceled was because the other individual preferred to get her information through email. Karen knew this and found Susan to be highly responsive, often sending Karen a reply through email in the evenings.

"I told Ken that Susan found it easier to do her best thinking away from the office. Unfortunately, his response to this explanation was that *he* didn't like sending emails."

The message that wasn't getting through to Ken was that if he wanted to work effectively with Susan, he was going to have to communicate in the way *she* preferred. Otherwise, he was always going to find that their meetings were canceled because other, more pressing items were getting in the way—at least for her.

This example raises a number of issues around effective communication and transparency that speak to how often we misread others' intentions. It was obvious to Karen that Susan thought she was being clear. By continually canceling each of their meetings, she believed she was sending a clear message that face-to-face meetings with Ken every week weren't a priority for her. Ken, however, just wasn't getting that message. And because of that, he was likely to make assumptions about Susan's motivation for canceling. There was a risk he would conclude that the other manager didn't like him, or wasn't interested in his project. You can see how, with this kind of misalignment in their relationship, Ken and Susan weren't managing to work together effectively during normal times, let alone have confidence that they could ride the heat curve together when the going got tough.

That's why a few years ago, Karen's team at Clorox worked on ways to drive home the message that everyone needed to "assume good intent."

Karen explains: "What I could see is that a lot of conflict came from misunderstandings like these. People misread intent all the time. Whenever such a challenge occurred, I had to counsel my people to ask: 'What else do you think could be happening?'"

I am always suspicious when I hear leaders attribute someone else's actions to one driving goal or intent, as in "they just want more power." Karen tries to look at multiple factors. "I've been surprised at how eye-opening it has been for my team when I've helped them understand how broader social and emotional factors play into people's behaviors."

This goes beyond simply being more open with others. It would be easiest if Susan would simply say, "Sorry, Ken, meeting face-to-face every week doesn't work for me. Could you please use emails instead so I have time to give greater thought and consideration to what you're asking? I do care about your project, I just do not have time during the day to meet with you now."

There can be many reasons someone may not feel able to be so clear. To really be open to others' best intent requires developing greater *empathy* for other people and what might be behind their behavior. Karen adds, "I try to step back and think through what other people might be feeling and why they might dig their feet in. That helps me develop greater empathy for that person. When before, it was just banging heads from opposite sides of the table. It's the empathy that causes someone to metaphorically move around to the other side of the table and sit beside the person they would otherwise have a problem with."

"What else might be happening here?" is an excellent question to ask when looking to develop resilient relationships with members of other teams, who might not know you very well—nor you them. Without having a basis of trust to begin with, it's easy to jump to conclusions as to what others' intentions are. But, as Karen advises, when other managers and members of their teams are behaving in a way that we consider unhelpful or even downright obstructive, it's invaluable to ask yourself what else could be causing their behavior. Could they be distracted by something you're not aware of? Maybe something else is going on in their professional or even personal lives that might be putting them under pressure. When others don't appear to have time to talk to you, as was the case with Susan and Ken, it's wiser not to jump to conclusions about it being personal or the result of disinterest, and to consider whether other issues are taking priority. Then it's up to you to try and find out how to overcome this impasse.

Yes, one of you has to be the "bigger person." And since you have educated yourself in the way of resilient relationships, this is something you will need to take on board—at least in the beginning. Someone has to reach out, it might as well be you.

Make Deposits Before Withdrawals

We've already mentioned the adage that likens relationships to bank accounts, in that you have to make deposits before you can make withdrawals. This strategy lies at the heart of what the leaders we talked to rely on to build resilience across all of their internal company relationships.

As Stig pointed out, "If you spend your life making deposits and continually giving to people, there's a point at which they get it and understand that that's who you are."

Stig uses this to good effect in his business relationships, especially with other members of organizations who might not know him as well as his own team members. While it can appear unfair to be the person who is always giving and not getting much back, Stig sees this as an investment that pays off in the long term.

"People will be more offended if they don't know you and you make a mistake, than if they *do* know you and what your character is. This involves you making consistent deposits. You won't see a difference in the first week or the first month, or perhaps even the first year. But over time, people get what you're about."

Not only do you need to embrace this level of flexibility with your interdepartmental relationships, but they must also be strong in terms of the effort you put in and the results you achieve. Just as in exercise, like yoga or Pilates, so too in relationships—the stronger your roots, the more flexible you can be. The leaders I've come across always want their organizations to be meritocracies: places where hard work and results have the most currency. Within the resilience model, you'll remember that "strong" is defined as creating value for both parties. As Stig says, "I've always felt like doing more than my share, which is how I get other people to start developing the same kind of values. And you know, it's contagious."

Which brings us back to intentions.

If you see an action by someone else in your organization, but misunderstand the intent of the action, your relationships are likely to be more tenuous and susceptible to breakdown under stress and pressure. And if everyone in your organization is also accustomed to this reactive approach, everything you do will become more dramatic, political, and less resilient when the heat is on.

Help other people to know you will be fair, in terms of giving them the benefit of the doubt and not jumping to negative conclusions about their intentions. Let them see you are strong with respect to wanting to create value for all sides. That's how you help to create relationships across your organization that will thrive.

Stig adds, "It's all about people knowing your intentions before you come into the room. If your intentions are, 'If a hole needs digging I'll pick up the damn shovel and dig; I will help you,' then they'll likely bail you out if you need bailing out. But if you don't deserve it because you haven't put in your part, then they probably won't."

As I intimated earlier, because resilient relationships are all about the *dynamic*, it's up to you to provide a model for others to follow so that you can begin to make an impact well beyond your own team.

Karen at Clorox has developed some practical strategies for dealing with this issue as she works cross-functionally to improve innovation and accelerate product development throughout her organization.

"We expect people to behave very rationally, and that's where I think a lens of 'How do I interpret what you're doing and the intent that lies behind that?' is helpful."

She tries to suspend judgment and be open to a wide variety of reasons for someone's actions. "Some of the activities that I've spent most of the time on with my teams involves trying to sort through others' behaviors and understand those relationships by stepping back and looking at multiple factors: what do *they* need to get out of this project? What does this project mean to *them*? This is their baby. How is this going to make or break this business and *their* role in the business?"

Again, it's all about developing greater empathy and understanding. Which is something that Karen needed in spades in one relationship she talked about.

Don't Sweat the Small Stuff

One leader Karen needed to work with was a rising star with a large sphere of influence in her group. The challenge for Karen arose when this man began resisting an important change that was required to ensure their teams were increasingly innovative. Unfortunately this man—we'll call him Sam—not only did not buy into or trust the new model that was being proposed, he seemed reluctant to trust Karen or believe the changes would drive the results needed. This gave him the excuse not to execute on the plan and do nothing about implementing it.

Karen realized that it was better to be flexible and meet *his* needs, rather than judge them or focus on her winning this battle. "I thought we could agree to disagree. But as I worked with him I understood that he wasn't okay with this. He needed to win me over; needed me to concede." Now, you may recognize these kinds of situations yourself. Ones where you are willing to take the high road and give way, not because you feel you need to pander to the other person, but as a means of building a bridge between you.

In Karen's case with Sam, her intention was to take responsibility for building and maintaining that bridge, rather than erecting an even stronger wall. Similarly, you may find in your interdepartmental dealings that some people seem not to have an intention to help build that bridge. You then have to decide what you can do to initiate a conversation to discover what's really going on for them. And then you can determine who among you has a bigger interest in maintaining that bridge. When it came to her dealings with Sam, it was obvious to Karen that her interest in bridge-building was what was going to hold this relationship together.

You might sum it up this way (and this is a topic that I've covered earlier in the book): the "us" and "them" mentality. A healthy tension can too easily turn into a battle. Maybe between sales and marketing? Between the operations people and the folks in finance? This notion of "the enemy within" can cause a lot of damage. Unfortunately, in corporate America, too many people give in to the fear response that lies behind much of this "us" and "them" divide.

I'll get more in-depth about how fear scuppers relationships with those outside of your organization, which also applies to those we deal with inside too. In the meantime, I'll close this chapter by pointing to the fact that the two leaders we interviewed and highlighted in this chapter—Karen Adamson of Clorox and Stig Nybo of Transamerica Retirement Solutions—both exemplify an approach to relationships that has helped them contribute meaningfully to the resilience of their organizations. Each has worked very hard to develop such inclusive attitudes. Again, it all boils down to intentions. In this case —what are yours when it comes to positive interactions with others throughout your organization?

Here are two final thoughts from each of our interviewees before we move on:

Karen: "With people like Sam, I hold a deliberate intention to work with them. To create a connection around other things and to show interest in what they're doing, which includes having cordial interactions when we pass each other in the hallways. Otherwise Sam might mistake me rushing by because I need to get to another meeting quickly as coldness; that I'm harboring a grudge. I've got to know him well enough to realize he wants everyone to be happy. Understanding those needs of his—drawing on my empathy—has helped considerably."

Stig: "If you look at all of the relationship books that talk about how to develop strong relationships, much of it has to do with asking people about their personal lives: How many kids do they have? What are their names? What sports do they play? That is a good technique— and I emphasize the word *technique*—for understanding who someone is and endearing yourself to that individual. But if there isn't genuine caring behind it, that becomes all too obvious and can backfire.

"Where I'm technically very poor at the former—I don't do a great job of asking about the kids, or knowing what sports they like—what I do a good job of is caring about people. And I think that comes through. I try and project to people throughout our organization, such as someone who works in operations that I only talk to once in a while, that when I smile and ask how things are, I really mean it.

"So my point is that there are two approaches to consider: knowing about someone's family versus really caring about them. I'm not saying either one is bad. Both are good. I just focus on the one I'm naturally good at. But both of them work, because both take effort. And people appreciate effort."

Chapter Eleven

CREATING RESILIENT RELATIONSHIPS IN A COMPLEX RELATIONSHIP ECONOMY

Back in the 1990s I was working with a well-known networking company at the top of their game: fast growth, loved by Wall Street, famous CEO, and a marquee client to have on your client list. Competition to work with them was fierce, so when we won the account I felt I'd bagged a trophy client, one that would be a source of revenue and referrals for years to come.

The problem was, this company had taken their success too much to heart and had become arrogant and harsh. For example, they would treat our support staff, and sometimes our consultants, very poorly by not responding to calls or emails, or sounding angry when they did. I'd go so far to say they showed disrespect and made the kind of unreasonable, last-minute requests none of our other customers made. They might have thought themselves strong, but they were neither flexible nor fair; dealing with them wore everyone out.

After checking with other firms, I learned this was the networking company's reputation and standard procedure: they bullied their vendors and were known for coercive relationships. One vendor said they were secretly happy they lost the account to us, and offered his "condolences" to me for winning the account!

They did seem to value the actual work we did, but we eventually had to part company. Before we ended the engagement, one of my staff complained about the "abuse" they regularly received from this client, and someone pointed out: "I know it's bad for us, but imagine how bad it must be to work there? They treat each other this way as well!"

Eventually other competitors were able to come into the market by matching this company's technology, but treating their employees and customers much better. Finally, humbled by poor financial performance, they chose to mend their ways and improve their external relationships. While they are now still successful, their previous culture came at the cost of a smaller market share with almost no growth.

The lesson here is that even if you have a better product and great market position, you can still lose out if your external relationships are not resilient.

Which brings us to the key question: how can you take the tools you've already used with your team and your cross-organizational relationships and direct them toward building the right kind of relationships with clients, customers, vendors, and other external partners? In today's volatile and uncertain world, you need to create relationships where you will still be "the last person standing" when the going gets tough.

But first, let's look at how relationships like these can be set up to be resilient. Then we'll explore what you can do when the heat is on and the resilience quotient of those relationships is tested.

You're Not Closing a Deal, You Are Starting a Relationship

Karen from Clorox has learned that you can definitely work with people who share your values—as long as you change your focus from price or cost to shared interests: "What you're trying to do externally is feel out where the common interests lie. The more you can be explicit around where those interests are and how you meet each other's needs, the faster you can build a relationship that actually meets those needs," she notes. "If you dance around it too much, or if you're trying to get your needs met without actually understanding what the other side's needs are, you're never going to have a really resilient relationship."

Alan Armstrong, CEO and founder of Eigenworks, agrees that resilient business relationships are built on this foundation of underlying shared interests, not on product or price alone. "Wise buyers share this information and smart sellers insist on learning and addressing underlying needs, even if the buyer seems to be focused on price and terms."

This way, the relationship is set to be strong from the start, which also makes it easier to be flexible and fair because both sides are looking to find mutually beneficial outcomes.

This kind of focus works especially well with today's subscription business model, where the focus is on an ongoing relationship rather than a one-time purchase agreement. The way to win in this new relationship economy is to build resilient relationships that lead to what is often called "customer success." Yes, customer satisfaction is no longer enough!

Welcome to the Relationship Economy

But, practically speaking, how can you actively focus on the client's interests? One example that Alan points out is the way some companies are looking at their customer usage data. If the customer is not using certain features of the product, for example, they will proactively reduce the customer fee, such as when the customer has paid for a premium version but is only using the basic features. Team communication software company Slack goes one step further and will automatically suspend payments if they notice that one of their clients is not using the system—such as when they are on vacation.

"Slack describes it as part of their core value of empathy," says Alan. The current Slack policy[24] is as follows:

> "Most enterprise software pricing is designed to charge you per user regardless of how many people on your team are actively using the software. If you buy 1,000 seats but only use 100, you still get charged for 1,000. We don't think that's fair. And it's also hard to predict how many seats you'll need in advance.
>
> "At Slack, you only get billed for what you use. So you don't pay for the users that aren't using Slack. And if someone you've already paid for becomes inactive, we'll even add a pro-rated credit to your account for the unused time. Fair's fair."

That's certainly not just fair but very generous on the part of Slack. But there's another side to this, too. Because buyers also have a big part to play in making sure their relationships are more resilient—by becoming "generous buyers." By that I mean someone who learns what is in the seller's interests, which may not always be limited to financial gain. Consider how the seller might also value referrals or be able to use the client in marketing materials, or find ways that the client can serve on their advisory board. There are any number of creative ways that broaden the opportunities for each party to add value to the other, and contribute to a strong, flexible, and fair—resilient— relationship.

---

24 "Pricing," Slack, accessed December 20, 2015, https://slack.com/pricing.

Do this *before* you're immersed in the heat of conflict and potential fear of change and you'll find it much easier to sustain the compassion and empathy you would otherwise feel for your clients, vendors, and partners. This is also the best way to ensure you keep them on board when the going gets tough.

Karlin, CEO of Sloan Group International, has learned how to set up her client relationships to be more resilient, while also growing her company and competing in a tough marketplace. "We tend to have long-term relationships with clients and I think being really explicit about our values has been very profound."

She makes sure to understand the client's values and expectations, so there are fewer chances of "breakdowns" up ahead, adding: "We'll get to know people pretty well and have a big commitment to not being high-pressured salespeople, but being really a resource. If the client wants a transactional relationship where we're the vendor and it's a case of: 'Hop to it—get me my laundry list of things. I want a coach in Kazakhstan who's certified in the Hogan, and I want them yesterday'—that's actually a real example—then we will not be a good fit, because that's not the way we work."

Nevertheless, Karlin will always risk climbing the heat curve to see if there is a deeper values match: "When we get an unreasonable request, we need to be able to tell the client 'Well, we don't have access to everything on your list, so let's talk about your priorities and let's figure it out together.' We're much more interactive and collaborative. But if somebody just wants an order-taker we tell them it will not be that useful to work with us."

Know Your Value, Not Just Your Price

Alan of Eigenworks has interviewed over 2,500 buyers to learn how and why they make their purchasing decisions. He has found that "most salespeople operate from a place of fear and insecurity, so they avoid the heat curve and say yes to everything." This has the impact of turning that salesperson into an "order-taker" and not a partner. Alan says, "They will be too quick to discount the price as the way of closing the deal."

Later, the client will expect to always get what they want, and now the vicious cycle has been set up. So, if the sales person enters into the process without a sense of their own strength, then flexibility and fairness become even harder to achieve.

As Alan points out, "The primary problem that salespeople have is the imbalance or perceived imbalance of power between the buyer and the seller. You know, the phrase 'the customer is always right' is sort of an aphorism. But a lot of sellers/salespeople feel that they have very little power in a sales negotiation. They don't necessarily know if they're differentiated from other players, and this sets up an inequitable, unbalanced conversation between buyer and seller. This lack of strength impacts your ability to be flexible, because if something goes wrong in the buying/selling discussion, it's very hard for the salesperson to recover."

Alan suggests the typical sales culture found throughout many organizations can be a barrier to resilient relationships. "I think psychologically, sales is a profession that encourages insecurity, because you're measured by your number and you're only as good as your last month or your last quarter in traditional sales cultures." Yet there are three kinds of value that salespeople bring to the table, Alan explains: "First is their personal expertise; second, the product that they are delivering has value to the customer; third, the company they represent carries a vast amount of resources that can help this customer, whether that be through educating or helping make changes in the buyer's world."

This might be a good point at which to pause and really think about how your salespeople or business development are regarded, both inside and outside of your organization. Are you doing everything you can to ensure they know their value and are able to confidently communicate it to external partners? You can only *give* strong, flexible, and fair to your external relationships if you have developed it internally to begin with.

Give Compassion to Get Compassion

But let's be honest here, even a well-launched business relationship can go sour and may need help to avoid breakdown. So how do you handle such an experience? Karlin offered this story about achieving a breakthrough.

"I've had the experience of working with people who I feel are so fear-driven they've become rigid and afraid they're going to lose their job or lose credibility. I think you can get so rigid you forget that business should be about problem-solving and collaboration.

"We had a 'breakdown to breakthrough' situation with one of our clients, a young woman tasked with working with us to implement an enterprise-wide executive coaching program, who had no experience in the field. She seemed very scared, because this was big, high-profile job for her; on top of which, the CEO was watching her every move."

Like some newer managers under stress, this person thought she could succeed by treating Karlin and her firm the same way she was being treated. "Because of the position she found herself in, this woman really wanted to say to us, 'Here's what we're doing, do it;' to be the boss and prove her dominance. Internally, my team engaged in a lot of discussions about how we would feel if we were in her shoes. We looked to see what we could do based on that instead of taking the easy way out and simply complaining that she was a pain in the ass."

Rather than mirroring the same rigidity and fear-based behavior she was facing, Karlin choose to be as generous and compassionate as possible. She and her team focused on being as collaborative and interactive as they could, consistently solving problems and helping the client prioritize her needs. It was through these efforts that she successfully shifted the relationship from breakdown to breakthrough. "You can find solutions if you take the higher ground and always assume people are trying their best, and to look for what *you* can do to make them more comfortable."

It became obvious to Karlin that the lack of trust being shown by this young woman was really more about her lack of trust in herself. She was merely projecting how she felt internally onto those over whom she felt she had some degree of control. As more experienced, mature individuals, Karlin and her team had long figured out that few people are willing to be vulnerable and say, "You know what, I need to look good. Please help me look good." You have to take that on board and do whatever it takes to achieve that outcome on their behalf, even when it's not explicitly stated.

By changing her goal from protecting herself to helping her client, Karlin was able to use the strategy of "moving from doubt to trust" from Chapter Four.

"We could have easily sabotaged that relationship, had we not thought about it more deeply, because in that environment of fear it was impossible to have a real conversation about anything. But she reacted really well to being treated like a person, because she was this young woman in a high-profile job, and saw that we were being really nice and helpful to her; after a while, she understood what we were doing. But this didn't happen instantly. It required a long-term investment in that relationship."

But what do you do when that kind of approach doesn't work? In that case you have two options, advises Karlin.

"The first option is to shift the ground rules of the relationship so we are not expected to do the impossible but can actually meet their needs and become what they're asking for. The second option is to say, 'You know, we're not a good fit, and here's our partner company who might be able to help you.'"

That might be easy to suggest but is often hard to do when you're trying to grow and compete. As Karlin says, "A lot of this comes down to worldview. If your worldview is that whether it's a fit or not, you're going to be okay, that's very different to thinking, 'we must retain our customer base at all costs.' It's the latter view that makes you fear-based, defensive, and is bad for business over the long-term."

Give Trust to Get Trust

Jerry Michalski is the founder of REX (the Relationship Economy eXpedition), a think tank focused on accelerating our shift to a more humane economy. He believes that the best leaders and organizations build resilience into their external relationships by integrating trust into their business model.

"If you design from trust, you will build a different thing," he explains. But what does it mean to "design from trust"? Jerry provided a few examples. The facilitation methodology called "Open Space" is one example of designing from trust, in this case meeting design. For those unfamiliar with this term, Open Space[25] is a meeting system that does not involve creating any agenda prior to a meeting, but rather inviting people to attend if they are interesting in the topic, and then allowing the participants to create the agenda on their own, during the meeting itself.

Jerry explains, "Open Space says you can trust that the people who choose to come to the meeting are geniuses and that they'll determine what are the most important things to talk about."

You might recognize this as analogous to open source software, where rather then building walls and setting up security systems to keep their programming secret, companies share it openly with their users. Adds Jerry, "We trust that the code we're willing to share is not somebody's

---

25 For more on this method read *Open Space Technology, A User's Guide* by Harrison Owen (San Francisco: Berrett-Koehler Publishers, 2008).

asset and is actually *more* valuable because we've all worked on it and sorted out the bugs. That way we can all build for-profit businesses on top of it."

Another effective strategy Jerry suggests is what he calls "gestures of trust." A good metaphor for the concept is the simple tradition of shaking hands. Jerry says, "The handshake is an historical gesture of trust. It shows you I don't have a weapon in my hand and it causes us to touch, which creates some degree of physical bonding."

Think of what the LEGO Company did in 2015. They had just introduced a programmable chip in their toy and someone hacked into it and was installing their own code. Rather then try to shut this person down, they chose a gesture of trust.

"Somebody at LEGO woke up and said, 'Hey, wait a minute, we probably can never shut down everybody doing this kind of thing. It's probably a lot of fun. What if we work with this energy?'" says Jerry. "So they let that person in and that created a more resilient company. One of the payoffs of collaborating with people who you might initially see as your antagonists was this huge ecosystem with their customers."

What a Long Resilient Trip It's Been

One of the most resilient relationships in business has been the decades-long relationship between rock band The Grateful Dead (and its various incarnations since the death of leader Jerry Garcia) and their fans. The relationship is strong because their live concerts provide multiple sources of value: not only a place to enjoy great sound and lights—for which they spare no expense—their concerts are gatherings, which provide a unique sense of community the fans could not get anywhere else. They are flexible by performing across the US, providing many more chances for their fans to see them than other bands and using multiple channels for tickets, increasing the odds of each fan getting to see at least some of their always sold-out shows. The Dead have always been very fair to their fans even when it came to their most important asset: their songs. Rather then try to control all their intellectual property, the band encouraged and supported their fans making and sharing their own "tapes" (now digital files) of their concerts. They designed from trust by allowing their fans to share the music, as long as they did not make money off the content. Like LEGO, they let customers *into* the system so they could create their own value. Since what we create we own, this approach resulted in fans seeing themselves as co-creating the experience of being a Deadhead.

This was clearly a gesture of trust and vulnerability, since it offered a way for customers to use the product without paying. But what if everyone just traded tapes and never purchased the music? It turned out that in return for trusting the fans, the Dead were (and still are) rewarded by fans who continue to sell out their shows and still purchase music from the band. To this day the Grateful Dead—in their many post-Garcia versions—is one of the most financially successful bands in rock and roll.

It all boils down to the responsibility that a leader assumes, and the risk they are willing to take, according to Jerry. "If I choose to be *undefended*, I am not *defenseless*. It can also mean I believe I can defend myself pretty well; I've just dropped my guard. And dropping your guard is both a gesture of trust and an act of vulnerability." For a rock band, letting people bring recording equipment to your shows is definitely lowering your guard. However, the Dead have been known to aggressively pursue anyone who is abusing the rights they have shared, either with the music or merchandise. They will not allow sale of copyright materials on-line, for example.

Let's not forget, however, that for many organizations, and in some industries, creating this willingness to be that vulnerable is especially difficult. As Jerry says, "We have a lot of political organizations where it's really hard to swim in shark-infested waters. And there are some companies where that's just the culture: the leaders retreat within their culture of attack and assault and everybody's at each other's throats. In other places, it's the industry where that's the prevailing culture—in which everyone is job-hopping and looking out for their own advantage. I hear this a lot in the entertainment industry, for example. That's where things like gestures of trust can make a huge impact, because it's completely unexpected and different to the norm." Gestures of trust like the ones made by the Grateful Dead, LEGO, or Slack, for example. Jerry says, "That's a way to tell the consumer that you're already on their side."

When we are in an environment where there is high risk associated with gestures of trust, wise leaders take these chances in measured ways, and from a position of strength and flexibility. For example, the Dead might not have been able to allow taping of their music if they were not already selling out every show.

I have learned that when I look back on the best of my external relationships, giving before getting, trusting to be trusted, and caring so others will care has proven to be the best approach. Not because I always get my way, but because when I do not get what I want, I know I have my values intact, I can learn from the experience and then move on. This is the essence of a collaborative strategy implemented in an unsafe world. I sum it up this way: "I am not against anyone, but I am for myself." This means I have my own goals that I want to achieve, but I do not need anyone else to lose so I can win. Being more vulnerable, but only doing so when I have assessed the risk and reward, allows me to win in a competitive world while still living out my values and creating a brand that will attract others who believe as I do.

We began our journey looking for ways we could create resilient relationships on our own, without depending on others. You now know that even with critical external relationships, if you design your relationships to be strong, flexible, and fair, they will survive whatever "heat" they're subjected to and continue to draw strength, flexibility, and fairness from all parties involved. Having said that, we need to be realistic and recognize that in some cases it's better to end a relationship (or sometimes to not embark on it at all!) than be exploited. And each one of us can make that choice. So we have now come full circle; it really is up to each of us to choose to take the actions we need to build resilience into *all* of our business relationships. If you make that choice, the payoff will be profound: for your business, your leadership, and your life.

Now let's turn to our final chapter to summarize the key tools and strategies for moving from breakdown to breakthrough.

Chapter Twelve

OVERVIEW: KEY STRATEGIES AND TOOLS FOR RESILIENT BUSINESS RELATIONSHIPS

I t's so easy when you come to the end of a book like this, to close it, hope for the best, and trust that everything you've just learned has been embedded. You know that's not the way true mastery of a new skill happens. As I pointed out earlier, it takes much more than that, including continually reminding yourself what's essential versus a distraction, and gradually putting it into daily practice.

I thought I'd make this a bit easier for you by capturing the key concepts from each chapter into a final overview. The insights you'll find here will also facilitate sharing these ideas with your team or colleagues in other parts of the business, or kick-starting valuable conversations with your external business partners. Because we all want to ensure that, when the heat is on (as it seems to be constantly these days), none of us devolves into breakdown mode. We need as many breakthroughs as we can get!

Introduction

Relationships in business matter much more than most people think when they start a career. Those leaders who know how to create relationships that hold up under stress and heat will succeed over others more focused on their own technical talents or the need for short-term financial results. These leaders are too focused on themselves: their ideas, their goals, and their power. Most of us take too long to learn how to focus on other's ideas, needs, and talents. As our environment becomes ever more volatile, uncertain, complex, and ambiguous ("VUCA"), our relationships must become even more resilient to survive. The days of pushing others around to get your way are over, and you will only be successful up to a point without eventually mastering relationship skills.

Chapter One—The Power of Resilient Business Relationships

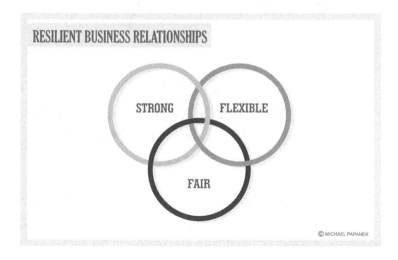

Resilient relationships have three key attributes. Use them to both evaluate and improve how you collaborate with others:

1. Strong: the relationship creates more value than what is contributed by both parties individually.
2. Flexible: the relationship continues to achieve the desired results and value for all sides, even under conditions of stress and change.
3. Fair: everyone feels that the benefits that stem from the relationship are distributed equitably and ethically.

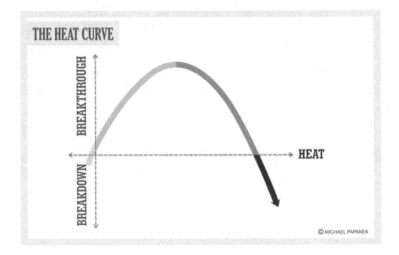

Remember the heat curve? This simple graphic can help you assess just how much conflict, passion, difference, and excitement each of your relationships can handle before it dips into breakdown mode.

When you consider each of your business relationships, look at which of them has a tendency to encourage breakthroughs and which do not. Be aware of which of them naturally transform the higher intensity of tension and stress into greater creativity and meaningful interactions, and which relationships quickly devolve into breakdown mode once the situation becomes too "hot."

Chapter Two—How Change Happens

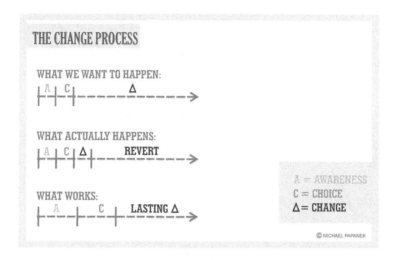

When we implement change in our organizations, or ourselves, we expect it to last. But all too often it doesn't because the culture pushes us to revert back to previous behaviors, especially in times of stress. Remember that lasting change follows three phases:

1. Awareness or "unfreezing": a period in which a person is provoked and motivated to recognize his or her own motivations, strengths, and weaknesses clearly. They become better able to understand how others perceive them and why their actions sometimes lead to unintended outcomes.

2. Choice or "reforming": the person is able to make new decisions and practice new behaviors that better align with their intentions, desired outcomes, and values.

3. Change or "refreezing": in which the leader has successfully made a permanent shift in the way they act and the outcomes they bring about, which are not detrimentally affected by adverse pressure.

Chapter Three—Getting to Why

"Motivation" is one of those abstract words that consultants and executives bandy about and which means very little unless it's related to something personally and emotionally meaningful. This is why you must create your own vision of how resilient you want your business relationships to be. You might call this your "leadership brand." If you fully committed to the exercises offered in this chapter you will be better positioned to create a sustainable future in which resilient business relationships play a key role.

Chapter Four—What's the Problem?

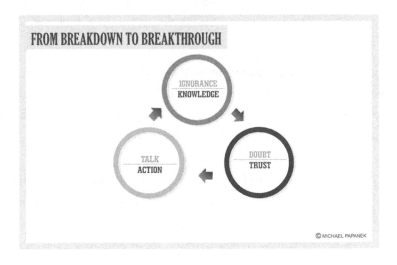

Use the following three strategies to help shift any business relationship toward greater resilience. Moving from:

1. Ignorance to Knowledge is the act of increasing mutual understanding of the whole person. It's time to stop thinking of others merely as functions (e.g. "housekeeping") or roles (e.g. "supervisor"). Each one has a personal history, goals, and

concerns that are unique. How much do you know—really know—about the people you work with?

2. Doubt to Trust is the act of taking a calculated risk that exposes you to increased dependence on the other party. As you will have discovered from the case studies and personal stories shared throughout this book, this is a risk well worth taking. Not only does it prove your intentions are relationship-focused, but the very movement from doubt to trust will help to reveal the intentions of the other party, through the way they react to your willingness to trust them.

3. Talk to Action involves *showing* rather than simply telling someone what you value or believe in. How often have you told someone that actions speak louder than words? But to what extent are you living that advice yourself?

Chapter Five—From Ignorance to Knowledge

The foundation of any resilient business relationship is a deep level of understanding and connection. Otherwise it's too easy to "fill in the blanks" with incorrect or self-serving assumptions. This first strategy in the breakdown to breakthrough process involves ensuring each one of you shows empathy for the other: your challenges, goals, and values.

It's hard to appreciate this before you actually make the effort, but when you open yourself up to others they will usually open up to you. Remember what Will Schutz wrote in *The Human Element*: "You cannot go anywhere new until you tell the truth about where you are."

Chapter Six—From Doubt to Trust

I know that very few of us enjoyed calculus, so don't get too hung up on the look of this "trust formula." But it's perhaps the simplest way I know to illustrate how this sometimes-opaque process works:

$$T = \frac{f(I \times C)}{Risk}$$

Where:

- Trust (T) is the decision you make when you determine that it's safe to give power over your interests to another person. This determination is "f," or a function of three other factors:

- Intention (I) or *evidence* of what is driving the other person's behavior (as opposed to your assumptions or beliefs). Do they appear to have your best interests at heart, not just their own? Are they transparent in the way they communicate the reasons for their actions? Note that as "I" increases trust increases as a consequence.

- Consistency (C) in terms of how frequently someone's actions match his or her words. Do they regularly meet their commitments? Do they keep these commitments under changing circumstances, especially ones involving stress and difficulty? Again, as "C" increases trust increases. (Note that if either I or C is zero, there cannot be any trust.)

- Risk speaks to what is at stake if the relationship succeeds or fails. How stable is the environment? How well can you predict what is likely to happen? Remember, risk is the *context* in which trust happens. The bigger the risk, the more Intention and Consistency you will need to build that trust.

Chapter Seven—Talk to Action

When faced with tough times, we all too often focus on "what can I *say*," rather than "what can I *do?*" While it's tempting to keep trying to use different words and terminology during a breakdown in communication, the better approach is to stop talking and let your actions speak instead. If you really value a customer or employee or business partner, are you showing it—or just saying you value them? This strategy can be more challenging to implement than others, but may have the biggest payoff of all.

If you haven't done so by now, it's time to take an audit of your actions to see if you have opportunities to *show* (i.e., *live*) your values rather than talk about them. If you really are committed to achieving buy-in from others and want to develop more resilient relationships, you need to influence others to get involved.

Chapter Eight—Shifting the Heat Curve

This was the point in the book when we focused on *implementation*, and I asked you to select a key business relationship so you could practically apply the strategies for improving it. The key steps for implementation are:

1. Assess the current state of the relationship: what is happening now, and how does the relationship reflect the three key attributes of strong, flexible and fair? What is the state of your heat curve today?

2. Determine the key gaps: based on the above assessment, where should you focus so that you will have the most impact? Which strategy or strategies did you decide upon (you did do the exercise, didn't you)?

3. Take action: this meant applying the strategies through "action learning," involving trying to make a change and then assessing the impact of that new commitment. But it's not a "one-time" deal. You will need to repeat until the relationship has improved in the way everyone wants it to.

Once again, you were provided with a set of simple, powerful worksheets that will guide you through the process. If you haven't used them yet, I strongly suggest you do so now. Either on your own, or to guide your meetings with the team members and other business colleagues and partners. That's what taking action means. *Doing something*, not just reading about it!

Chapter Nine—Leading a Resilient Team Culture

Once you were comfortable with your own abilities to establish and nurture resilient relationships it was time to "scale up" and learn how to apply the process to your team. We learned from some very effective leaders the importance of:

1. Having an "I've Got Your Back" culture. This means focusing on supporting each other rather than competing or viewing "the enemy within." Intra-team attacks are not tolerated. Leaders who do this soon see the benefits (better, faster decisions, with more accountability for results) in having created an environment that engenders more trust, risk, and innovation.

2. Hiring for relationships. By placing greater importance on relationship skills in the interview process, you can ensure that new team members will thrive in your "I've Got Your Back" team culture. This includes involving existing team members in hiring decisions to build ownership for the new hire's success, before they even come on board.

3. Building resilience in meetings. These events are a reflection of your team culture and soon show how strong, flexible, and fair your relationships really are, as well as how well you ride the heat curve. By reinforcing a supportive culture and removing yourself (as the leader) from the center of your universe, you'll inevitably find that other team members step up, take more ownership of relationships, and can handle more heat while performing to the best of their abilities.

Chapter Ten—Resilient Relationships Across the Organization

Having accomplished resilient relationships within members of your own team, it's time once more to scale up. This time the focus was on breakthrough relationships with other people in your organization. Cross-functional relationships are often the weakest link in many organizations. Yet when an organization is taxed by radical change it is the resilience of these interconnecting relationships that results in survival—or otherwise. Some of the strategies our interviewees used to build effective relationships with other teams and functions include:

1. Focus on intent: Rather than attributing simplistic and selfish motivations to other people's behavior, our leaders suggested becoming open to other possibilities, including actions based more on emotional than rational reasons. If you can understand the real, complex reasons driving someone's behavior, you can find an area of common ground on which to create a breakthrough.

2. Don't sweat the small stuff: too often people lose sight of the more important outcomes and can become focused on getting everything they want. Your colleagues—even those you may not appreciate very much—have their own accountabilities and some give-and-take should be expected.

3. Show me. It is more important to really *care* about people than to have a gift for building instant rapport. Your actions over time—those that show you care—will be more respected than an annual, computer-generated birthday card or remembering someone's spouse's name.

Chapter Eleven—Creating Resilient Relationships in a Complex Relationship Economy

We are entering a period of global commerce that some have called "the relationship economy." Old business models that were built on command and control have been turned upside down to allow for new relationships between companies and consumers, buyers and sellers, and competitors and suppliers.

These relationships are not only more important, but they're even more complex. In fact, the resilience of your key business relationships is tested every time someone creates a new disruptive business model. Our interviewees suggested a number of ways to ensure your most important relationships survive this constant heat:

1. Know your value. Whether you are a buyer or seller, your focus needs to be on building a value-based relationship from the start. Sellers should know their value and be confident in what they bring to the table. Buyers should be clear and open about what they want, not just how much they want to pay. Your strength lies not just in your price or product, but in how you can work together with others to create optimal, breakthrough results.

2. It's not me, it's you. Yes, I'm going to come out and say it one more time: sometimes you may have to "fire the client" or otherwise end a relationship that is proving more trouble than it's worth. If you have tried to meet their needs and have found the client does not share your core values, try not to let financial goals keep you tethered to this no-win situation. How do you avoid getting yourself in this position in the first place? Go back and re-read point number one, above.

3. Let down your defenses. If you can be open and ready to let others in, you can turn a threat into an advantage. It has been

my experience, in more than thirty years of corporate life and consulting—as well as the experience of all the interviewees who shared their insights for this book—that gestures of trust and transparency are rewarded with loyalty and resilience. This is especially true, and even more important, when tough choices need to be made.

Change can be a lonely endeavor. My final advice is to reach out to others to help you and you will find you reach your goals so much faster and more easily. That includes reaching out to me, your author! I am eager to hear about your trials and successes and help you build a career and be the kind of leader you will be proud of no matter how much heat comes your way. Your investment in your relationships will pay off more than any other investment you make.

MICHAEL PAPANEK

Experience/Background

Michael Papanek is Principal and Founder of Michael Papanek Consulting. Michael has over thirty years of expertise leading successful large-scale change initiatives and increasing the performance of people and organizations in complex, competitive markets.

Michael works with senior leaders facing new challenges, due to either an expanded role, new business targets, new strategies, or other key change initiatives, mostly in large organizations and fast-growing high tech companies in complex global markets.

Part coach, change agent, facilitator, and tool-giver, Michael helps leaders and their teams think more strategically, accelerate their own growth, and improve their influence while having more fun and increasing their resilience.

Michael guides leaders to increase their self-awareness through "action learning" so the leader can choose how best to leverage their strengths to promote employee accountability and collaboration, especially when the leader is in a new or expanded role, has new goals to achieve, or is member of a new leadership team.

Prior to becoming an Organizational Change Consultant, Facilitator, and Leadership Coach, Michael gained his high-tech experience working in various technical and leadership roles at EDS, the global IT services company.

Michael has also led sales teams, large-scale IT transformations, product development, sold and managed engagements for Fortune 100 organizations, facilitated strategic planning, and led leadership development programs globally for Interaction Associates, the global leadership development company. Michael also served as General Manager for Learning Innovations and was a member of the Board of Directors at Interaction Associates.

Michael is an avid sailor who enjoys racing and cruising in the SF Bay Area and around the world.

Clients

- Agilent
- Apple Computer
- Bureau of Land Management
- Chevron
- Cisco Systems
- Clorox
- Core-Mark
- eBay
- Earth Justice
- Electronic Arts
- Facebook
- Google
- GE Capital
- Head Start
- Hewlett-Packard
- Johnson and Johnson
- Kaiser Permanente Health System
- Levi Strauss & Co. Microsoft
- Moody's
- NetApp
- National Academy of Sciences
- Oakland Unified School District
- San Francisco School District
- Silicon Graphics, Inc.
- Sprint

- Southern California Edison
- Sutter Health System
- Tektronix
- Texas Instruments
- US Forest Service
- VMware
- Wells Fargo Bank
- Yahoo!

Education/Trainings/Certifications

- BS, Economics - The University of the Pacific
- Graduate Work (Management and Information Technology)— Wayne State University and the University of Michigan Ross School of Business
- Member—Bay Area and National Organizational Development Network (NODN)
- Certified Coach: Realise2™—A strength-based leadership assessment system
- Certified Coach and Trainer: The Nine Doors™—A personality assessment / accelerated growth system
- Certified Master Trainer in workshops for Coaching, Leadership, Teamwork, Facilitation, Conflict Resolution, Change Management, Strategic Leadership, and Organizational Change

Contact Information (I would love to hear from you!)

michael@michaelpapanek.com
www.michaelpapanek.com

DR. LIZ ALEXANDER

Dr. Liz Alexander's gift and talent lies in guiding clients to communicate in ways that intrigue, influence and positively impact their target market, leading to business growth and sustainability. Since 1984, when her first book was published in the U.K, she has authored or co-authored 17 internationally published nonfiction books, many of which are best-sellers and have attracted multiple international awards.

Liz maintains resilient relationships around the world. Born in Scotland, she was raised in England and moved to the U.S. in 2009. She currently lives in Austin, Texas, visits India on business several times a year, and her co-founder of boutique consultancy, Leading Thought (www.leadingthought.us.com) is based in Sydney, Australia. She acts as book strategist and consulting co-author to senior executives and entrepreneurs globally (www.drlizalexander.com), and is Special Counsel, Book Strategist & Writer for Senate SHJ, Australasia's largest privately-owned PR firm.

BIBLIOGRAPHY

American Psychological Association. *Stress in America 2009*. Accessed June 11, 2014. https://www.apa.org/news/press/releases/stress/2009/stress-exec-summary.pdf.

Appleyard, Frank. "Empathetic Doctors Have Better Treatment of Diabetes." The Mayer Institute, March 10, 2011. http://www.themayerinstitute.ca/empathetic-doctors-have-better-outcomes-in-the-treatment-of-diabetes/.

Barnes, Barry. *Everything I Know about Business I Learned from the Grateful Dead: The Ten Most Innovative Lessons I Learned from a Long, Strange Trip*. New York: Business Plus, 2012.

Barrett, Ann, and John Beeson. *Developing Business Leaders for 2010*. Conference Board, April 2002.

Bazelon, Emily. "How to Stop the Bullies." *The Atlantic Monthly*, March 2013.

Blacksmith, Nikki, and Jim Harter. "Majority of American Workers Not Engaged in Their Jobs." Gallup, October 28, 2011. http://www.gallup.com/poll/150383/majority-american-workers-not-engaged-jobs.aspx.

Bryant, Adam. "Google's Quest to Build a Better Boss." *New York Times*, March 12, 2011. http://www.nytimes.com/2011/03/13/business/13hire.html?_r=0.

Buckingham, Marcus, and Curt Coffman. *First, Break All The Rules: What the World's Greatest Managers Do Differently*. New York: Simon & Schuster, 1999.

Castellano, Stephanie. "Decision Science." *Training and Development Magazine*, July 2014.

Dean, Roger. "Bring ... Me ... A ... Rock!" *persuasive INK*, 1998.

Demaray, Michelle Kilpatrick. "Why Do Some Kids Cyberbully Others?" *The Wide Wide World of Psychology* (blog), *Psychology Today*, April 26, 2013. http://www.psychologytoday.com/blog/the-wide-wide-world-psychology/201304/why-do-some-kids-cyberbully-others.

Dittmann, Melissa. "What Makes Good People Do Bad Things?" *Monitor on Psychology* 35, No. 9 (October 2004): 68.

Eichenwald, Kurt. "Microsoft's Lost Decade." *Vanity Fair*, July 31, 2012. http://www.vanityfair.com/news/business/2012/08/microsoft-lost-mojo-steve-ballmer.

Fisher, Roger, and William Ury. *Getting to Yes: Negotiating Agreement Without Giving In*. Edited by Bruce Patton. New York: Penguin Books, 1991.

Forum Corporation. *Driving Business Results by Building Trust: Leadership Pulse Survey*. 2013.

Gladwell, Malcolm. *Blink: The Power of Thinking Without Thinking*. New York: Back Bay Books, 2005.

Graham, Alan, Kevin Cuthbert, and Karlin Sloan. *Lemonade: The Leader's Guide to Resilience at Work*. Veritae Press, 2012.

Guthridge, Liz. "Why 'SAFETY: Zero Injuries' Succeeds and 'Speak Up for Safety' Fails." *Connect Consulting Group* (blog), June 24,

2014. http://connectconsultinggroup.com/why-safety-zero-injuries-succeeds-and-speak-up-for-safety-fails.

Hurley, Robert. "The Decision to Trust." *Harvard Business Review*, September 2006.

IBM Institute for Business Value. *Leading Through Connections: 2012 IBM CEO Study*, May 2012. http://www-935.ibm.com/services/multimedia/anz_ceo_study_2012.pdf.

Interaction Associates. *Building Trust in Business 2012: How Top Companies Leverage Trust, Leadership and Collaboration*, June 2012.

Ketchum Inc. *Ketchum Leadership Communication Monitor*. May 2014.

Kleiner, Art. "The Cult of Three Cultures." *Strategy + Business*, July 1, 2001. http://www.strategy-business.com/article/19868?gko=04205.

Lewin, Kurt. *A Dynamic Theory of Personality*. New York: McGraw-Hill, 1935.

Lewin, Kurt. *Resolving Social Conflicts: Field Theory in Social Science*. Washington, DC: American Psychological Association, 1997.

Luscombe, Belinda. "Why E-Mail May Be Hurting Off-Line Relationships." *Time*, June 22, 2010. http://content.time.com/time/health/article/0,8599,1998396,00.html.

Marrow, Alfred J. *The Practical Theorist: The Life and Work of Kurt Lewin*. New York: Basic Books, 1969.

Nisbett, Richard. *The Geography of Thought*. New York: Free Press, 2003.

Owen, Harrison. *Open Space Technology: A User's Guide*. San Francisco: Berrett-Koehler, 2008.

Pink, Daniel. *Drive: The Surprising Truth about What Motivates Us*. New York: Riverhead Books, 2011.

Rock, David. "Why Organizations Fail." *Fortune*, October 23, 2013. http://fortune.com/2013/10/23/why-organizations-fail/.

Schutz, William. *The Human Element: Productivity, Self-Esteem, and the Bottom Line*. San Francisco: Jossey-Bass, 1994.

Schutz, William. *The Truth Option: A Practical Technology for Human Affairs*. Berkeley, CA: Ten Speed Press, 1984.

Senge, Peter, Art Kleiner, Charlotte Roberts, Richard Ross, and Bryan Smith. *The Fifth Discipline Fieldbook*. New York: Doubleday Currency, 1994.

Sinek, Simon. *Start with Why: How Great Leaders Inspire Everyone to Take Action*. New York: Portfolio, 2011.

Sloan, Karlin. *Unfear: Facing Change in An Era of Uncertainty*. Self-published and printed by CreateSpace, 2010.

Smith, Abby. "Is the Leadership Trust Gap Hurting Employee Engagement?" Forum, November 11, 2013. http://www.forum.com/blog/the-leadership-trust-gap/

INDEX

Page numbers in *italics* indicate figures.

Printed in the USA
CPSIA information can be obtained
at www.ICGtesting.com
JSHW022335140824
68134JS00019B/1501

9 781630 479800